North Hudson Regional
Fire & Rescue
1999-2009

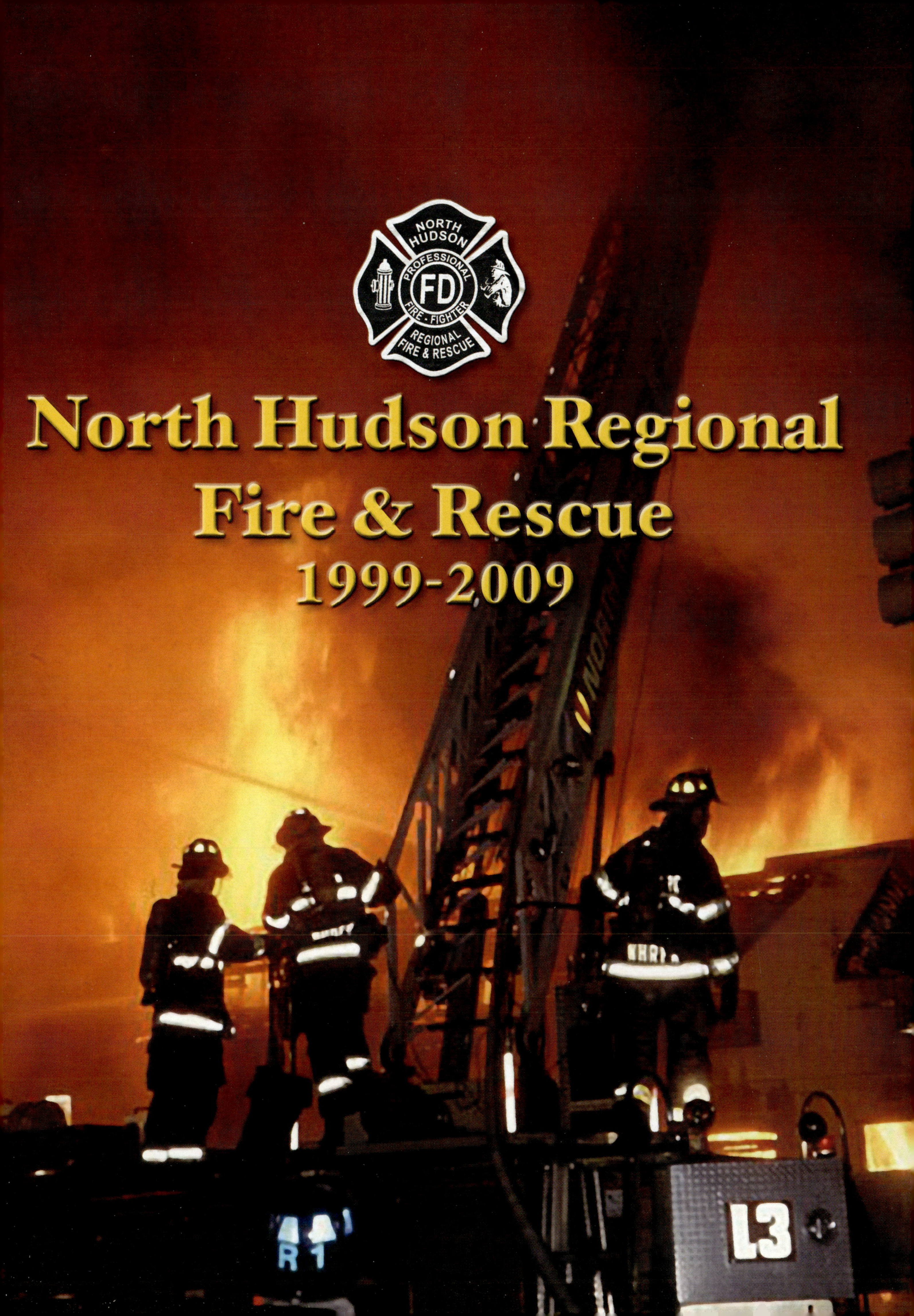

M.T. Publishing Company, Inc.
P.O. Box 6802
Evansville, Indiana 47719-6802
www.mtpublishing.com

Copyright © 2010
North Hudson Regional Fire & Rescue

Graphic Designer: Elizabeth A. Dennis

All rights reserved. No part of this publication may be translated, reproduced, or transmitted in any form or by any means, electronic or mechanical, including photocopying and recording, or by any information storage and retrieval system, without expressed written permission of the copyright owner and M.T. Publishing Company, Inc.

The materials were compiled and produced using available information; M.T. Publishing Company, Inc., and the copyright owner regret they cannot assume liability for errors or omissions.

Library of Congress
Control Number 2010931396

ISBN: 978-1-934729-37-3

Printed in the United States of America

Contents

Fireman's Prayer	4
Chief of Department	5
NHRFR Yearbook Committee Co-Chairman Duane	6
NHRFR Yearbook Committee Co-Chairman Morrison	7
President of PFA of NJ and President of NHFA	8
Fireman's Mutual Benevolent Association President	9
Presidents of North Hudson Fire Officers Association	10
Past Chiefs of North Hudson Regional Fire & Rescue	11
Acknowledgements	12
Badge 343	13
Headquarters Plaque	14
In Memoriam	15
Vincent Neglia	16
Firefighter's Memorial Park	18
NHRFR Fire Department Histories	20
West New York Fire Department 1889-1999	22
North Bergen Fire Department 1924-1999	26
Union City Fire Department 1925-1999	34
Weehawken Fire Department 1861-1999	40
Guttenberg Fire Department 1873-1999	43
North Hudson Regional Fire & Rescue 1999-2009	47
Notable Incidents Published in Fire Engineering Magazine	58
Night of Fire	68
North Hudson Regional Fire & Rescue Badges	70
North Hudson Regional Fire & Rescue Personnel	71
NHRFR Fire Companies & Units	100
Honor Guard Members	150
Honorary Battalion Chiefs	152
Front Pieces	153
Friends of the Fire Service	154
Chief Presutti's Last Day	156
Sergeant Alvarado Serving in Iraq	157
Wrapping Party	158
Hospital Visits	160
Christmas Parade	162
Charity Dodgeball Tournament	164
M.D.A. Boot Drive	166
T-Shirts For Troops	167
Johnson Turner Golf Outing	168
Training of the Dominican Republic Fire Department	170
NHRFR In Print	172
Fire Prevention	174
NHRFR Families	176
NHRFR Yearbook Committee	188
Firehouses Closed	189
Name Index	190

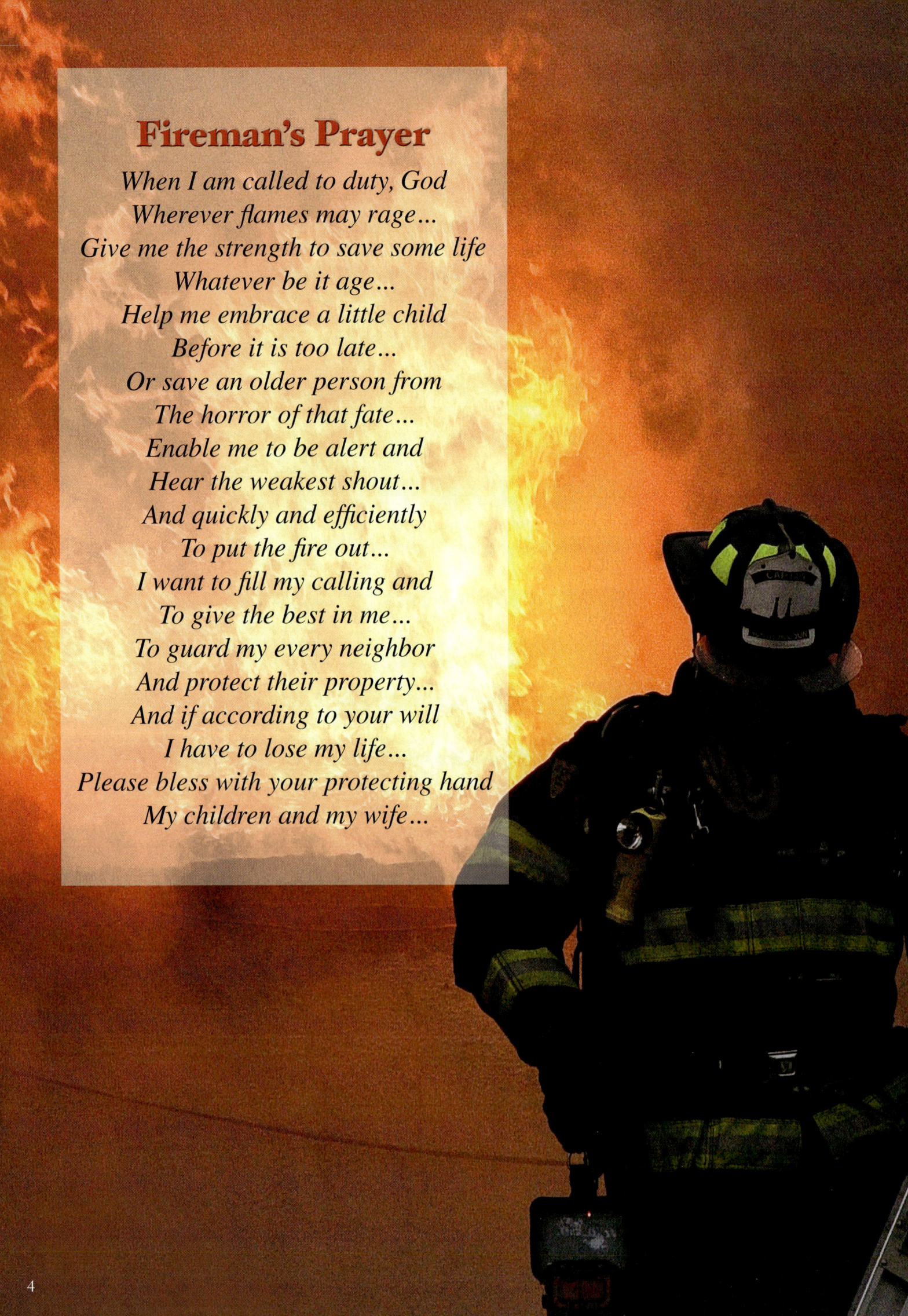

Fireman's Prayer

When I am called to duty, God
Wherever flames may rage...
Give me the strength to save some life
Whatever be it age...
Help me embrace a little child
Before it is too late...
Or save an older person from
The horror of that fate...
Enable me to be alert and
Hear the weakest shout...
And quickly and efficiently
To put the fire out...
I want to fill my calling and
To give the best in me...
To guard my every neighbor
And protect their property...
And if according to your will
I have to lose my life...
Please bless with your protecting hand
My children and my wife...

Chief of Department

NORTH HUDSON
REGIONAL FIRE & RESCUE

11 PORT IMPERIAL BOULEVARD • WEST NEW YORK, NJ 07093
(201) 601-3542 • FAX: (201) 330-2699

As the first yearbook goes to print, I extend my appreciation to all the members of North Hudson Regional Fire and Rescue, as well as members of the previous five fire departments, for their dedication and professionalism. While North Hudson Regional has a short ten year history, its foundation lies in the long and proud traditions of the predecessor departments of North Bergen, Union City, Weehawken, West New York, and Guttenberg. Our roots are firmly anchored in the traditions of the previous departments, and those departments continue to exist in the hearts and minds of members who once served proudly in them.

Just as the "birth of a nation" over 200 years ago became known as a melting pot, North Hudson Regional is a melting pot of prior departments and of members from different cultures, talents, abilities, and ideas. Just as that nation was forged into the greatest country in the world, North Hudson has forged itself into a truly great, progressive fire department.

Brion W. McEldowney

North Hudson Regional Fire & Rescue was born on January 11th, 1999. It is a Department that was based on change, and what a change it has been. Throughout this period of change the knowledge, experience, and skills of the members have made North Hudson Regional a well rounded and effective fire department.

We have come a long way in the last ten years. We have learned new skills from each other. We've grown in our ability to accept new ideas and technologies. We've learned to accept the change that was cast upon us and make that change work to the benefit of those we are responsible to protect. We have met the challenges as they came, and constantly prepared for new challenges that are yet to appear. I have no doubt that the members of North Hudson Regional will continue to protect the public with a high degree of excellence and professionalism far into the future.

In our short ten year history, we have endured the best of times and the worst of times. The best of times was on every occasion in which our members excelled by making that "good stop", saving a life, receiving an award, or achieving a promotion. The worst of times was the passing of members, both active and retired. Of course, that ultimate worst of time was September 9th, 2006, the tragic day when our own, Firefighter Vinny Neglia, made the most extreme sacrifice that one man can make for another.

I thank the yearbook committee for their hard work and commitment to developing this ten year history of North Hudson Regional – a snapshot of the Department - and of the "best job in the world".

Sincerely

Brion W. McEldowney
Chief of Department

North Hudson Regional Fire and Rescue Yearbook Committee Co-Chairman

NORTH HUDSON REGIONAL FIRE and RESCUE YEARBOOK COMMITTEE

Robert J. Duane

It is with extreme pleasure that I welcome you to the 10th Anniversary Yearbook honoring our past and present firefighters, fire officers, fire dispatchers and administrative staff. As you proceed though the history of our past departments and present day North Hudson Regional Fire and Rescue; I am sure you will be both pleased and honored to be part of this yearbook.

As I personally reflect on my career with both the West New York Fire Department and the newly created North Hudson Regional Fire and Rescue, I must say that the wonderful friendships and acquaintance I have made and memories both wonderfully funny and sometimes sad are part of being a member of the brotherhood of firefighters. I consider myself very fortunate to wear the uniform of a firefighter and proudly stand among the bravest and most dedicated people to serve and protect the citizens of North Hudson.

I hope this 10th anniversary yearbook brings you both pleasure and fond memories as you also reflect on your own careers and as family and friends browse through the pages they will see the dangers and hardships we all have encounter in the past 10 years but also our accomplishments and successes in saving life and property in North Hudson.

Stay Safe,

Robert J. Duane

Battalion Chief Robert J. Duane
Co-Chairman

North Hudson Regional Fire and Rescue
11 Port Imperial Blvd
West New York, NJ 07093

North Hudson Regional Fire and Rescue Yearbook Committee Co-Chairman

NORTH HUDSON REGIONAL FIRE and RESCUE YEARBOOK COMMITTEE

The fire service has been a great learning experience for me. Having been brought up in the fire service, with two uncles on the job since 1960, for a total of seven family members in the fire service.

This book was a labor of love, that shows the past histories for the former five fire departments as well as the history of North Hudson, which have a history of pride and tradition.

Having gone from the West New York Fire Department with only 90 members to a Department like North Hudson Regional with over 320, was an overwhelming experience, but one I'd never forget.

Since the merger, a lot of new friendships have been forged, that may not have been possible if we had remained five individual Departments.

In closing, I hope you enjoy the contents of this book, which would not have been made possible without the talented skills and computer savvy of Kimberley Kingsbury, of Fire Headquarters. Thanks Kim!

Stay Safe,

Robert P. Morrison III

Captain Robert P. Morrison III
Co-Chairman

Robert P. Morrison III

North Hudson Regional Fire and Rescue
11 Port Imperial Blvd
West New York, NJ 07093

President of Professional Firefighters Association of New Jersey and President of North Hudson Firefighters Association

Dominick Marino

*Glen Michelin
1999-2009
Former President North Hudson Firefighters Association*

Brothers past and present:

I am honored to be able to contribute to this yearbook that remembers the members of the former fire departments that make up the North Hudson Regional Fire and Rescue, while it honors the present members. In 1998, as a member of the North Bergen Fire Department and the President of the North Bergen Fire Fighters, I remember firsthand the concerns that all the firefighters from North Bergen, West New York, Union City and Weehawken had because of the formation of the regional department. We were apprehensive that the traditions and memories of our individual departments would be forgotten. Over the last 10 years, we have been able to continue some of those traditions, have lost others and made new ones. It is our hope that this yearbook will memorialize our former departments while recognizing the new department and the "new" members who had no affiliation with the former departments.

This yearbook is a fitting tribute to our members who give unselfishly to the citizens of North Bergen, Guttenberg, West New York, Union City and Weehawken twenty-four hours a day, 365 days a year. To the second and third generation of firefighters, this yearbook will serve as a treasured memento. The North Hudson Regional Firefighters have always demonstrated exemplary loyalty to the citizens through their actions while on the duty and off duty.

I have the distinct honor of being the president of the North Hudson Firefighters and also the State President, representing IAFF firefighter's through-out the State of New Jersey. This book will serve as a powerful reminder to the communities that we serve and protect of the men who put their lives on the line for them every day. I am sure that all who read this book will enjoy this celebration of the North Hudson Regional Fire and Rescue and the former municipal fire departments.

I want to take this opportunity to thank and commend the members of the yearbook committee for the outstanding work they've done in producing this memorable yearbook.

Dominick Marino
President

Fireman's Mutual Benevolent Association President

October 23, 2009

To the Members of North Hudson Regional Fire & Rescue,

As the NHRF & R marks its 10th year in existence, the New Jersey State FMBA wishes to acknowledge all your members, who have served their communities with commitment and dedication. The members of the NJ State FMBA throughout the State will forever recognize the contributions of the firefighters who proudly served Union City, West New York, North Bergen, Weehawken, and Guttenberg.

Your professionalism and dedication in service to the citizens of your respective communities in the face of unimaginable bureaucratic turmoil and political chaos is a testament to the finest traditions of the fire service. Every member of the North Hudson Fire Department should be specially recognized for delivering vital life saving support in spite of the obvious challenges placed before them.

Please know that as North Hudson Regional Fire & Rescue moves into its next decade, every resource of the New Jersey State Firefighter's Mutual Benevolent Association will continue to be made available to further ensure the rights and safety of your members, who continue to inspire through your commitment to duty and by placing the interests of the citizens you serve above all else.

Fraternally,

William J. Lavin

William J. Lavin

Brian McGorty
1999-2004

Robert Duane
2005-2006

Brian Boele
2007-2008

James J. Stelman
2009-Present

Presidents of North Hudson Fire Officers Association

I Can Not Tell A Lie

It is with great delight that I write of the dubious honor of being the first President of the North Hudson Fire Officers Association. I say dubious because of the uncertainty of the times. Everything was a battle. There was fear of the unknown. Who could be trusted? How would we be represented and what was it we were seeking? We took a leap of faith or perhaps we realized that what we had in common was far greater than our differences. More importantly our internal battles were mere spats when compared to the need to protect our rights and secure an equitable future. Toward that end we were constantly in legal battles to clarify the gray areas that seemed to always be created by the Regionals use of smoke, mirrors and attorneys. As you can see things have changed greatly. We are now in constant legal battles over things that are clearly black and white but which the Regional chooses to ignore in their nostalgic longing for cloudy days of yore. But that is the nature of the beast and why I use the term dubious as a substitute for whatever word you may like to insert.

This brings me to the part about honor and having been the first President was truly that; an honor. The reason for that is much easier to explain. It is the guys. Strangers, thrown together under less than ideal circumstances, who embraced the Brotherhood of Firefighters and became a family. Granted at times we are dysfunctional and have our problems like any family. But when it really counts we have been there for one another. We have grieved together as we buried our own and we have shared the joys of births and marriages. We have crawled through intense heat and blinding smoke and after ten years have emerged on the other side better men because we did it together.

May the Angels Watch Over Us All

Brian McGorty, President N.H.F.O.A. 1999-2003

Past Chiefs of North Hudson Regional Fire & Rescue

Robert Jones Sr.
1999-2001

Anthony J. Presutti
1999-2001

Edward Flood
2001-2003

Acknowledgements

Dave Velez

With his meticulous "Felix Unger" style of photography and computer expertise for this anniversary yearbook's photo gallery, we'd like to thank retired North Hudson Firefighter David Velez for his time and assistance. Before Regionalization, Dave was a member of the North Bergen Fire Department.

In the late 1990s, a mutual aid running card assignment was established for automatic mutual aid, by the five municipalities (Weehawken, West New York, Union City, North Bergen and Guttenberg), which were dispatched by the North Hudson Communications Center (Fire Control) which was established in 1982.

Firefighter Velez was assigned to North Bergen Engine Company 2. In 1998, his unit was dispatched on a 2nd alarm assignment, to an apartment complex in lower Union City. His company was on the scene and operating before the uptown Union City companies arrived.

Firefighter Velez ascended the fire escape and a mother handed him her baby. Firefighter Velez started his descent down the fire escape's drop ladder, when the ladder separated from the fire escape.

Firefighter Velez cradled the baby to his chest and fell to the ground, landing on his SCBA. He and the infant were rushed to the hospital, where firefighter Velez was diagnosed with a broken back and the baby suffered no injuries.

After surgery and extensive rehab, Dave returned to full duty as a firefighter with the newly formed North Hudson Regional Fire and Rescue. He was assigned to North Hudson Engine Company 1, which was previously North Bergen Engine Company 2.

Due to the extent of his injuries, Firefighter Velez took a disability retirement. His love of the fire service has never faded and he remains active as a Fire Inspector for the Township of North Bergen.

Dave is also dedicated to serving the community by organizing the North Hudson Regional Christmas Wrapping Party and Hospital Visits, as well as taking photographs at numerous fire department events.

The yearbook committee would like to extend their greatest thanks to Dave for all he has helped us accomplish in putting this book together. Without his hard work and dedication this book would not have been made possible.

Kim, Bobby & Ronnie

Ron Jeffers

Back in high school, a teacher gave the class an assignment; it was to be a written report three pages long. When the time came to hand the papers in, one wise guy in the class handed the teacher a picture he drew, he told the teacher that a picture is worth a thousand words, and that a thousand words was three pages long. The teacher accepted his report.

A single photo really does have an impact on people. The three firefighters at 911 raising the American flag on a mound of debris that was once one of the towers; the fireman with the baby in his arms at the Oklahoma City Bombing of the Murrah Federal Building (April 19, 2000) or a picture of Vinny Neglia in the firehouses raising a glass with the saying "TILL WE MEET AGAIN."

Now imagine having a collection of photos from jobs you worked, whether you were on the job from one year or on the job for 35 years. There is such a history of jobs in photos from Ron Jeffers.

A retired Union City Sergeant, Ron can always be seen at jobs with his all access pass and his camera. Ron has a better record of accomplishment then the Post Office dark of night, rain, and snow; he is a real fixture on the fire ground. How many times have you come out of a fire building to change your Scott bottle and said "Hi Ron." When the time came to put together the North Hudson Regional Fire and Rescue yearbook, Ron was a must have, and he went above and beyond the call of duty, not only with his pictures but by becoming part of the yearbook staff.

Ron without your love of the job, this book would not have the impact we needed.

RON THANK YOU!

Badge 343
A Tribute To The 343 FDNY Firefighters Who Died September 11, 2001

When new firefighters have been hired and badge numbers designated, badge #343 has never been issued....it has been retired in the memory of those who perished on that fateful day in New York City.

My most memorable experience happened on September 14, 2001, while working at the World Trade Center. We were heading back to rehab after spending our third day on the pile. I radioed to command that I would stay behind while Captain Robert Agostini was being treated at the triage area for an eye injury. As I waited alone an old woman came up to me and handed me a plate of ziti with meatballs. I did not tell her, but we had just recovered a bunch of bodies including some firemen from Squad 18 and I was feeling a little disheartened. I immediately noticed that I was holding fine china and a silver fork. When I asked the woman where this came from she explained to me that she lived four blocks away and wanted to help. So every day she made a few meals and would feed about six emergency personnel during dinner time. Amidst all the chaos, devastation, and destruction I felt a moment of calmness and comfort, as if I were a guest in her house and she was a longtime friend. She will never know the impact that she had on me, but her act of kindness and humanity will stay with me until the day I die. To her and to the many who supported us I say Thank You.

Captain Sean Miick (Squad 1)
North Hudson Regional Fire & Rescue

North Hudson Marine 1 welcomes the U.S.S. New Yorker.

The U.S.S. New Yorker....some of the steel from the World Trade Center Towers was used in the making of this ship.

Badge 343 13

Headquarters Plaque

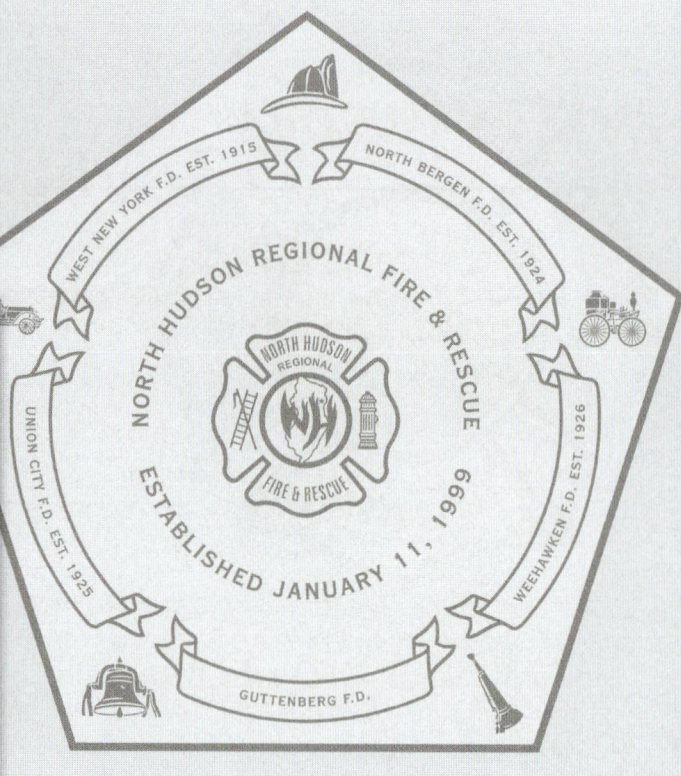

    I am pleased to be included in the North Hudson Regional & Fire Rescue 10th Anniversary Yearbook. During my tenure as the first Chairman of the Management Committee, I never forgot the tradition of the five regionalized Fire Departments and the communities they so proudly served.

    We owe a debt of gratitude to fire department personnel from the past, the pioneers who fought fires and engaged in emergency operations with what was available to them. When I became a member of the fire service in 1960 there had been very little change in our profession for many years. Protective clothing could still burn, self-contained breathing apparatus was still in experimental stages, communication equipment was not reliable and the technology we take for granted in our modern day departments had not been developed during those "early years."

    I am grateful to the management committee who acted swiftly on my suggestion to memorialize the firefighters of the five departments and the sacrifices they made protecting the property and citizens in their communities. I appreciate the cooperation of the Chief and Directors. The committee led by Battalion Chief Michael Cranwell did a marvelous job in designing the plaque which I am elated to mention, serves as a history of the past and present and preserves our tradition and heritage.

    I will conclude by saluting the firefighting forces and staff of our progressive regionalized department. I am proud to have been part of the endeavor, and the plaque properly displayed at headquarters will bring back many memories to all who view it.

Robert A. Aiello,
West New York Chief of Department (1980-1995)
Chairman of the Management Committee (1998-2007)

DEDICATED TO THE FIRE OFFICERS AND FIREFIGHTERS OF GUTTENBERG, WEST NEW YORK, NORTH BERGEN, UNION CITY AND WEEHAWKEN.

THEIR DEVOTION TO DUTY, THEIR DECADES OF BRAVERY, SACRIFICE AND SERVICE PROVIDE THE TRADITION UPON WHICH THE NORTH HUDSON REGIONAL FIRE & RESCUE HAS BEEN FOUNDED.

In Memoriam

In Memory of
Vincent Neglia
Michael Fischer
Joseph McLean
Kevin O'Driscoll
Carmine Flora

Michael Fischer

Joseph McLean Jr.

Kevin O'Driscoll

Captain Carmine Flora suits up.

Vincent Neglia
Firefighter Killed Searching For Victims In Union City

When North Hudson Regional firefighters arrived at a reported fire in a three-story wood-frame dwelling at 1813 Bergenline Avenue in Union City, shortly after 5 a.m. on September 9th, there was no smoke visible from the front of the structure. Fleeing residents told firefighters the blaze was on the second and third floors, and that there were people still trapped inside the building.

Firefighter Vincent Neglia raced up the stairs with his crew from first-due Squad Company 2 to search for victims. Above Neglia a fire raged that was concealed by a tin ceiling in the old structure.

Without warning, flames flashed through the ceiling, trapping the veteran firefighter under fiery debris.

Neglia's brother firefighters immediately rushed to rescue him, hitting him with water and pulled him out from under the debris. He was lowered to the ground through a rear window, where firefighters and EMS personnel applied CPR. He was in cardiac and respiratory arrest. Paramedics tried to revive him as the building erupted in flames; but, Neglia died soon after at St. Mary Hospital in Hoboken.

"There was no indication how serious the fire was burning when he entered the building," said Jeff Welz, co-director of the North Hudson Regional Fire Department, which covers this and four other municipalities. Several other firefighters were treated for non-life threatening injuries and went back to work.

16 Vincent Neglia

"He was the lead firefighter, which is why he was in the room first," Welz said. "The fire didn't present itself."

It was later discovered that all occupants of the burning building had escaped safely.

Firefighter Neglia started his career with the North Bergen Fire Department but became a member of the North Hudson regional department when North Bergen and Union City merged with West New York, Weehawken and Guttenberg in 1999 to form a single 300 plus member force. Normally, Neglia was assigned to Engine Company 13 in North Bergen, near the Bergen County border. Due to a battalion chief's test scheduled for that morning, captains taking the test were relieved from duty from their 24-hour tour that evening. Neglia was detailed to Squad 2 in Union City, located just a few blocks from the fire scene, to cover.

"Vinnie was very colorful," said Captain Joe Zavardino of Engine Company 13. "He made the days go fast."

Neglia often assumed the role of Santa Claus or an elf when firefighters delivered Christmas toys to local children. He enjoyed his Harley and flying a remote control miniature helicopter. The last time Fire Chief Brion McEldowney saw Neglia was two-days earlier when Neglia took it upon himself to lighten the chief's mood by flying his toy helicopter over Fire Headquarters on Port Imperial Boulevard.

Authorities believe the fire began in an air shaft that separates the three-story walk-up from another building next door, Welz said. The fire traveled up the air shaft and into a larger-than-normal cock-loft space. They believe Neglia and other firefighters apparently entered the room just as the cock loft reached "flashover" point.

"He was not a quiet person," the chief said. "He was going to make sure you knew his opinion. He didn't care who you were."

Firefighter Neglia was the first firefighter to die in the line of duty in Union City since 1977, and North Hudson's first death.

"The firefighters did a tremendous job, and I don't know what they could have done differently," Chief McEldowney said.

A carelessly discarded cigarette or match is believed to have caused the fatal fire.

Firefighter Neglia is survived by a daughter, his parents, a brother and three sisters.

Ron Jeffers
1st Responder News

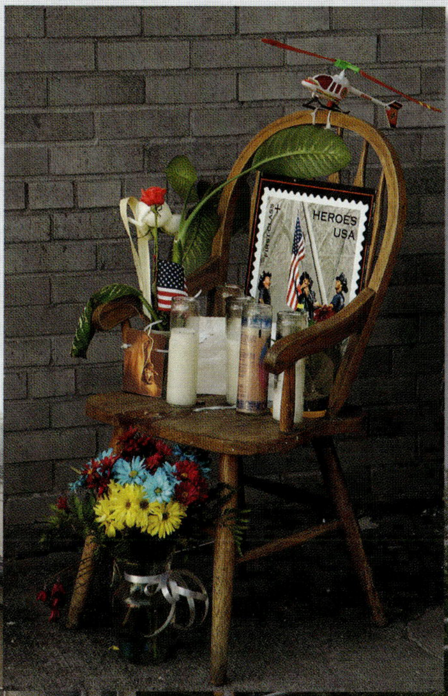

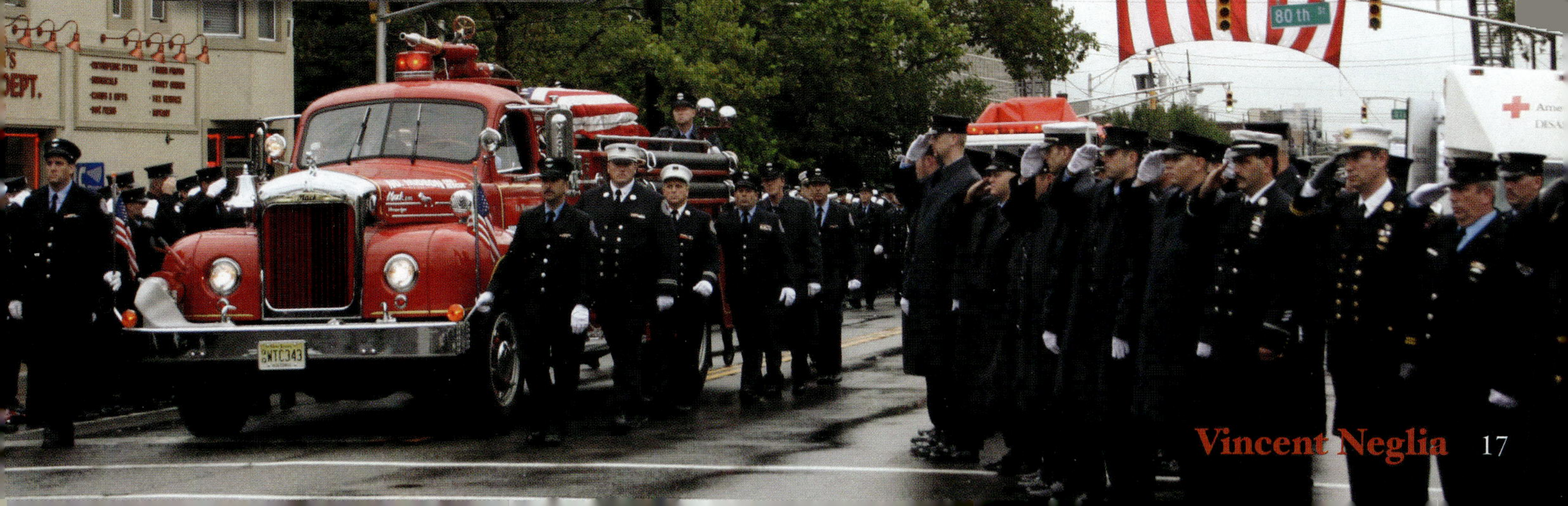

Vincent Neglia 17

Firefighter's Memorial Park
Union City, New Jersey

A long time project of New Jersey Senator and Union City Mayor Brian Stack was to create a new city park for the public to enjoy in this densely populated city, and to dedicate it to local firefighters. This dream became a reality on the morning of August 8th when a few hundred people filled Palisade Avenue near 9th Street for the grand opening ceremony.

The old Doric Temple building had outlived its usefulness and was costly to operate. With available funding programs, the building was torn down and a new park and swimming pool complex was open, built on the cliffs overlooking the Manhattan skyline.

Fire officials and the rank and file from the North Hudson Regional Fire Department, which now serves Union City, were in attendance along with firefighters from other Hudson County departments and EMS units.

At the entrance to the park is a monument. Facing west is a dedication to the fallen firefighters of the 9-11 attacks. Facing east is a listing of firefighters from the former fire departments that are now part of North Hudson that died in the line-of-duty in years past along with North Hudson Regional Firefighter Vincent Neglia.

Family and friends of these heroes were in attendance-some of those relatives now firefighters themselves. Firefighters from Union City, North Bergen, West New York, Weehawken and Guttenberg are listed. A replica of the North Hudson Regional shoulder patch is engraved in the middle of Palisade Avenue before the park's entrance.

Ribbon cutting by Union City Mayor, Brian Stack, (center) and city commissioners.

NHRF&R Honor Guard

North Hudson firefighters admire replica of the NHRF&R patch engraved in the middle of Palisade Avenue.

Firefighters Memorial Park at the top of the Palisades Mountains overlooking Manhattan.

Relatives of those firefighters listed on the monument stood behind Mayor Stack and the city's Board of Commissioners members as the ribbon was cut and the monument unveiled. Children, with their parents, lined up to jump into the new pool. Refreshment stands were also set up on the street.

As the ceremony ended, and children were entering the swimming pool, some of the on-duty North Hudson firefighters were dispatched to their fireboat to assist in the search and recovery effort involving the mid-air collision of a helicopter and small plane over the Hudson River near Hoboken.

A little over 12-hours later local firefighters were battling a fire that involved three buildings on 30th Street and Central Avenue in Union City.

Ron Jeffers
1st Responder News

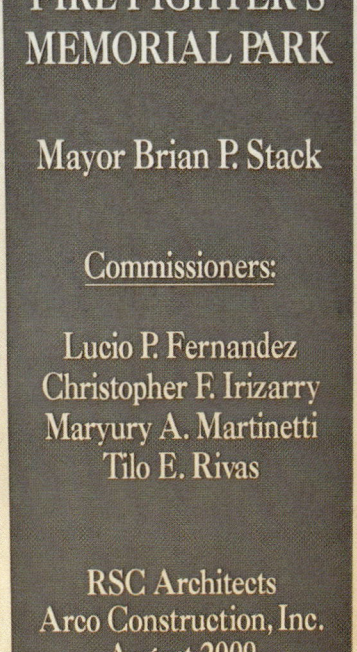

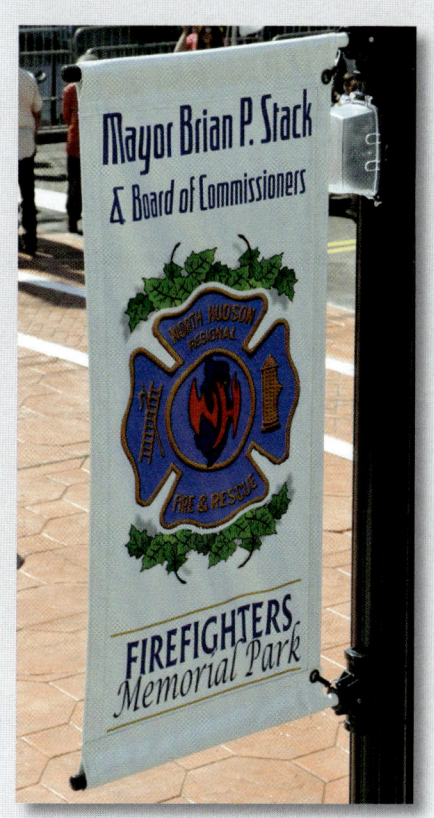

Firefighter's Memorial Park   19

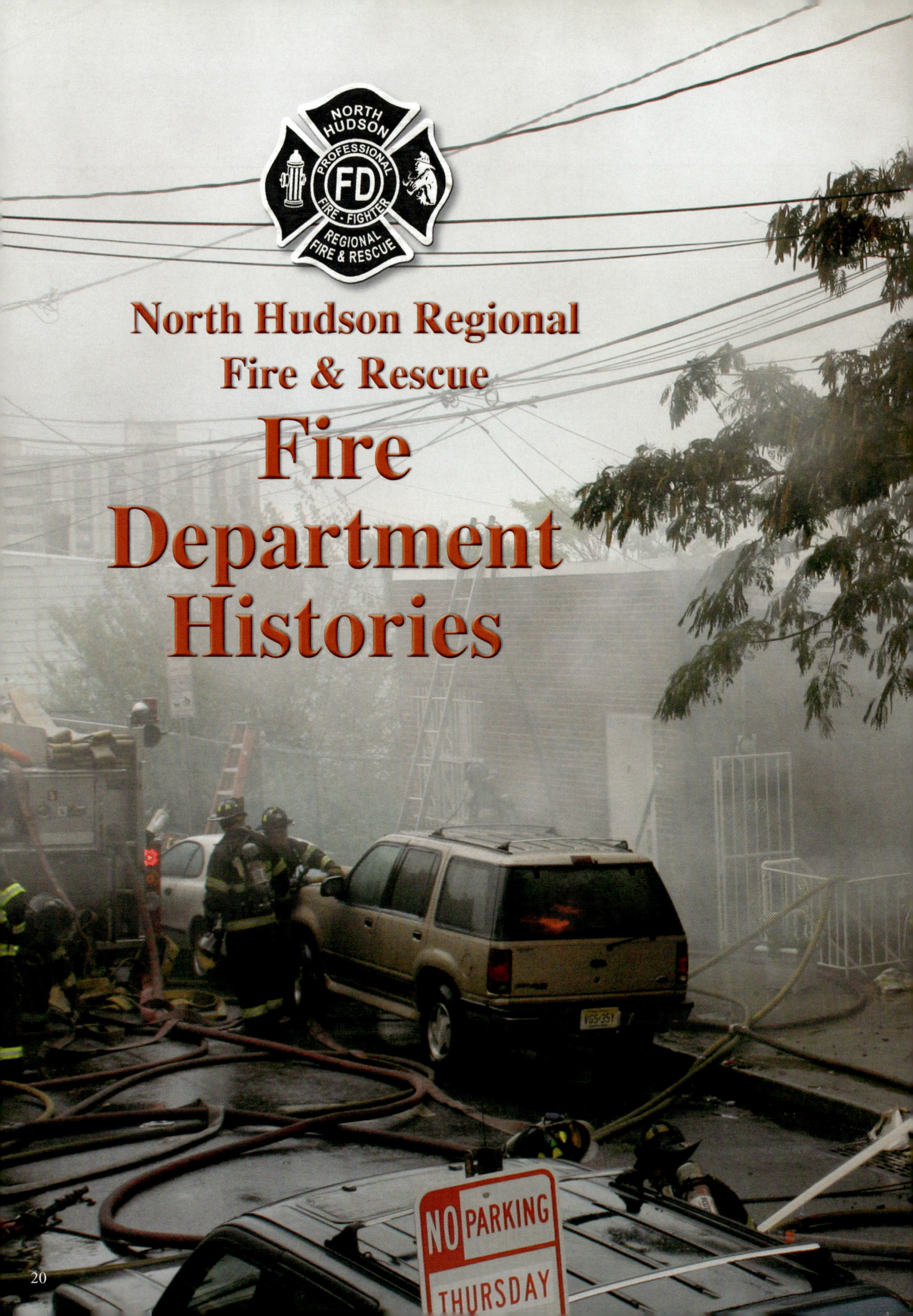

North Bergen 3rd alarm fire, 6810 Meadowview Avenue, November 1, 2007.

West New York Fire Department 1889-1999

Before Town of West New York was incorporated on July 5th, 1898, the first companies of the Fire Department were formed under the old name of Township of Union, back in 1889. The Department grew over the years to seven companies, which included one ladder, six engines and hose companies with over 300 volunteers, and 11 paid drivers by 1914.

West New York Fire Department 1914
Hickory Engine Company 1 organized 1889
Liberty Hose Company 1 organized 1890
Excelsior Engine Company 2 organized 1891
Enterprise Hose Company 3 organized 1901
Hudson Hose Company 4 organized 1906
Monroe Hose Company 5 organizer 1909
Empire Hook & Ladder Company 2 organizer 1889

The original hand pumped engines were gradually replaced with steamers starting with Excelsior Engine Company 2. Fire horses were the means of power to get the apparatus to the fires.

West New York Exempt Firemen's Association was organized on December 27, 1898, and continues to be a functional organization with regular meetings to this day. Active and retired members keep in touch at the Exempt Firehouse, formerly Excelsior Engine Company 2, at 6106 Polk Street. This is also the location of the West New York Fire Department Museum located on the second floor.

By the 25th Anniversary of the West New York Fire Department in 1914, all the temporary wood frame housing for the companies, which were either rented or borrowed, were finally replaced with their own brand new brick built firehouses. The following year, the West New York Fire Department became a fully paid department with three engine companies, two truck companies, one Deputy Chief and a Chief Engineer and a staff of 26 men. The five were designated as Engine Companies #3, #4, #5, and Hook & Ladder Companies #1 and #2. The volunteer department which had been serving the town up to that time was dissolved.

The Chief Engineer, later know as the Chief of Department, was paid $1,200 a year, Captains and Fire Alarm Electricians were paid $1,000 and firemen made $900 a year. On August 8, 1916 a new ordinance increased the department to 40 members and Engine Company #6 was established.

On February 10, 1920, the department went to a two-platoon system with an 84-hour work week. The Chief's salary was raise to $2500 a year and the position of Assistant Chief Engineer was created with a salary of $2250 a year. Two other posts were created: Mechanic at $2,100 and Superintendent of Fire Alarms at $2,100. Captains were raised to $2,000 and Firemen to

Emergency Truck

Truck 2 1925 American LaFrance 65-foot straight-frame ladder with tiller seat.

Engine 3's 1962 Howe Pumper.

1925 ALF Type 45 pumper, 1928 ALF Type 145 pumper, 1915 ALF Type 31-4 75-foot front-drive aerial ladder, 1916 ALF Type 20/14 city service ladder truck and 1926 ALF Type 31-6 65-foot front-drive aerial ladder.

In the 1950s, the Department employed four Ward La France 750gpm pumpers. In 1950, the Department placed into service its first tractor drawn aerial ladder-a Seagrave 3-section 100-foot model. In 1958 Truck Company #2 was disbanded and Engine Company #3 was relocated to their Hudson Avenue quarters. Engine Company #3's former quarters on Harrison Place became the reserve Truck Company #2's house.

In 1960, the department placed into service a Ford Emergency Truck at the Quarters of Engine Company #5 with one fireman assigned to it. In 1962, Engine Company #3 was assigned a Howe Defender 4WD 1250 gpm unit with high-pressure pump. This was a unique piece in the fact that only two of this style rigs were made by the manufacturer.

In 1970, Engine Company #5 was assigned a tilt-cab Ford C model Howe 1000 gpm pumper. Truck Company #1 was assigned a 1971 Howe/Duplex/ 100-foot Grove tractor drawn aerial. This rig was unique in the fact that only two units of this type were built by Howe. The second being purchased by North Bergen. In the same year, Engine Company #4 was assigned a Howe/Duplex 1250 gpm pumper.

In 1976 West New York joined the lime green apparatus color fad with the delivery of a Mack CF model 1250 gpm pumper at the cost of $60,000. The second lime-colored apparatus was delivered in 1979 and assigned to Engine Company #6. This was a Mack MB 1000 gpm model.

Tradition returned in 1983 when Engine Company #5 received a red Mack MC/Grumman 1250 gpm pumper that cost $118,000. In 1984 Engine Company #4's 1971's Howe/Duplex was heavy damaged in an auto accident with an under age driver. Firefighter Frank Zell was critically injured. Firefighter Frank Zell succumbed to his injuries some years later. The department had Engine Company #4's rig refurbished by Manhattan Towing in Ridgefield Park, New Jersey. It returned with two cross lay hose beds under the booster reels.

The Department received its first fully enclosed cab apparatus in 1985 with the delivery of a Spartan/Grumman 1250 gpm pumper that cost $167,550.

$1,600. The work week was cut to 67 hours by a 1946 ordinance and a November 15, 1950 ordinance further reduced the week to a 56 hour. In September 1966, a 42-hour work week was established with the addition of the 4th platoon. Fourteen new firemen were added that became know as the "Fabulous 14." New promotions added five Captains and one Deputy Chief to the department.

In the Departments history, the manning went from 26 men to 112 in the mid-1970s. At the time of regionalization, the manning was reduced to 81 members. During its existence, the W.N.Y.F.D. had five career fire chiefs. They were Ernest G. Becket, 1915-1950; Albert Schneider, 1950-1957; Charles F. Smith, 1957-1980; Robert A. Aiello, 1980-1995; and Anthony J. Presutti, 1995-1999.

The West New York Fire Department had a variety of firefighter apparatus in its history. An available list of apparatus from 1929 included: 1915 American La France (ALF) Type 31-4 75-foot front-drive aerial ladder, three 1917 ALF's Type 45 pumper's,

West New York Fire Department 1889-1999   23

In 1985, the yellow 1976 Mack CF pumper at Engine Company #3 was sent out to Grumman to be refurbished and repainted red. When it returned, it was re-numbered for reassignment to Engine Company #6. That same year the Department took delivery of a 1985 Seagrave 100-foot tractor drawn aerial. This apparatus was built on an older Seagrave "P" model cab in order for the rig to fit into the narrow bay door.

The Department sent their 1971 Howe/Duplex/Grove 100-foot tracker drawn aerial to Grumman to be refurbished in 1986, returning as reserve Truck Company #2.

In 1993, the Department received their first truly four door cab apparatus, with the delivery of two Emergency One Cyclone 1500gpm pumpers that totaled $433,576. They were the first 750-gallon water tanks, and the first to have company logos painted on the front of the cabs. Engine Company #4 was called "Border Patrol" and Engine Company #5 was known as the "Cross Town Express".

Ironically, in the late 1960's the West New York Police Department painted their radio cars red and white for better visibility and safety. In 1970 Engine Company #5, while responding to an alarm at 5809 Hudson Avenue, collided with one of these police cars at 61st and Jackson Streets. Engine Company #5 flipped over onto the officer's side. The police car was forced into the corner bar. All three firemen were thrown from the apparatus. Fireman Robert Pelletreau's leg caught under the rig. Off duty fireman Anthony Presutti ran over to assist and pulled his leg out of the boot which was pinned under the apparatus. Fireman Vincent Alessi was missing and initially thought to be under the rig. He was found a block away sitting on a doorstep in shock. The third fireman, William Voorhis, suffered a fractured left shoulder. Patrolmen Frank Schmelz was transported to North Hudson Hospital's Intensive Care Unit.

In the late 1970's Engine Company #5 and #6 collided at the same intersection sending all six firemen to the hospital with minor injuries and placing both rigs out of service.

West New York has had many major fires over the years from dwellings to commercial buildings to piers. On the evening of April 18, 1962, the eve-

Engine 3 was destroyed as a result of the coal docks fire in 1962.

Flames consumed everything in its path along the waterfront in 1962.

West New York Fire Department 1889-1999

Engine 4's 1971 Howe Pumper.

Fireman Joseph Liberton tried unsuccessfully to save Engine 3.

ning sky turned red due to a spectacular waterfront fire. The blaze caused an estimated $3,500,000 loss and went on record as one of the worst fires in the Hudson County area over the past 25 years. Box 425 was transmitted at 4:49 P.M. for a fire at the old Ontario and Western Railroad coal docks, which had been abandoned. When the first units arrived the flames, fed by dried wood and coal dust, were roaring through the old dock. The fire spread northward through Guttenberg and into North Bergen. A four-story building used for distributing vegetable oils was leveled.

For the next 5½ hours flames swept unchecked through the North Hudson waterfront destroying piers, huge vegetable oil tanks and at least ten barges. According to a Hudson Dispatch article, "Commissioner Edward Cavanaugh of the New York City Fire Department, at the scene to lend technical assistance, said it was one of the most devastating blazes he had confronted in his career."

Two West New York pumpers and a Guttenberg pumper were cut off when a wooden bridge they had crossed to get to the dock, burned behind them. Although they managed to get two of the engines to safety, West New York Engine 3's Ward La France pumper was completely destroyed by the flames. As the flames engulfed the apparatus, Fireman Joseph Liberton took an axe and tried to cut some of the hose lines to try to save Engine 3, but could not cut all of them in time to drive the pumper to a safe distance. He was forced to abandon the rig and suffered burns to his back, face and arms. In all nine firemen were injured.

On the evening of April 1, 1965, a passer-by walked into a neighborhood tavern and told the bartender that the lumber yard was on fire. The bartender said, "Yeah, I know- April fools." The passer-by said, "No!" At the same time, 7:15 P.M., other people were pulling street boxes 214 and 215 for a fire at West New York Lumber & Supply Company at 5105 Park Avenue. Some 400 firemen battled flames from Hudson County and East Bergen County. The intensity of the blaze, coupled with wind-blown flaming embers, prompted firemen to evacuate all persons living within a two-block area. Fallen power lines caused a blackout for an eight-block area, including North Hudson Hospital in Weehawken. Live wires landed on Truck #1 and firemen were ordered not to touch the rig. Initially, the lack of lighting caused no problem for firemen at the scene as the roaring flames lit up the area almost as bright as mid-day.

("*West New York Fire Department 1889-1999*" history submitted by Retired West New York Chief Robert A. Aiello, Retired Chief Anthony J. Presutti, Captain Alan Ballester, Captain Robert P. Morrison III, and Honorary Battalion Chief Ron Jeffers.)

West New York Fire Department 1889-1999

North Bergen Fire Department 1924-1999

Rescue 1's 1957 Chevrolet/H&H.

Engine 3's (Ex-4) Maxim Pumper.

History

The history of the North Bergen Fire Department is closely linked to the size and shape of the Township as well as its unique geological features of steep urban streets, large meadowland area and the industrial/ residential construction mixture. The Township of North Bergen covers 5.6 square miles. This is larger than the four other North Hudson Regional cities combined. North Bergen is the only city served by the North Hudson Regional Fire and Rescue Fire Department (NHRFR) to have at least one fire station in each of the departments' three battalions.

As with the other North Hudson communities, the North Bergen Fire Department began with volunteer firefighters using horse drawn fire pumps and ladders. When the department switched over to power driven apparatus in the early 1900's, it was still operated as a volunteer department. As the population of this urban area continued to grow, it was finally decided that the fire department would switch to a paid fire department in 1924. There was no chief of the new paid department until the appointment of Joseph A. McLaughlin as the first chief of the North Bergen Fire Department on February 1, 1929. Other members who rose to the rank of Chief of Department included; Warren Andes, Pete DiStefano, George Franke Sr., and George Viccaro. The last Chief of the North Bergen Fire Department was John DiPaolo. During the history of the department, there were also times when members performed as Acting Chief of Department. Some of these people were James Hargaden and Donald Barth.

Fire Stations

In bygone years, the fire stations in North Bergen each had a name. There was the Woodcliff Engine Company, The Overlook Engine Company, Paunpeck Engine Company, Peerless Engine Company, Eagle Hook and Ladder, as well as other names. After the formation of the paid department, the fire stations began to be known by numbers.

Engine Company 1, located at 62nd Street and Kennedy Boulevard, is now Engine 9 under the NHRFR. Through the years, this firehouse was known as a tight fit and a difficult house to back

1941 American LaFrance 75-foot tiller.

Howe Quad originally used in Rivervale was spare Engine 6.

Rescue 1 later became Searchlight 1.

North Bergen Fire Department 1924-1999

Truck 1's 1986 Maxim 100-foot tractor drawn aerial ladder.

into due to the buildings odd angle in relation to Kennedy Boulevard. However, many members mastered the art of Chauffeuring at Engine 1. Engine 1's radio call number under the North Bergen Fire Department was 661 and became nicknamed Big Red One. One fondly remembers Captain Ron Heitmann exclaiming on the radio "Big Red One is a signal 44." This fire station also housed the Deputy and his Aide. Under the North Bergen Fire Department, the Deputy's radio call number was car 667. Currently, this station is also the quarters of North Hudson Battalion 3

Engine 2, located at 9th and Paterson Plank Road is now Engine 1. It is the southern most fire station of the NHRFR. Engine 2's call number under the North Bergen Fire Department was 662. This old station underwent renovations in 1988, causing the Engine to have to ride out of Union City's 29th Street Fire Station until the restoration could be completed.

Engine 3 of the former North Bergen Fire Department changed locations several times over the years. It was located across from Franklin School at 52nd Street and Columbia Avenue. Then it was located at 69th Street and Tonnelle Avenue, across from the legendary Dolan's Bar and Grill. After the Township acquired the building of a former trucking company, Engine 3 was moved to 60th and Tonnelle Avenue. This location eventually became the site of the first Headquarters of NHRFR, although by that time, there was no longer an Engine Company operating out of the building. In 1994, Engine 3 was moved to the new station that spans from 43rd Street to 44th Street just off Tonnelle Avenue. This station was built with a unique drive through design. This fire station design was later utilized for NHRFR's new Headquarters Station on Port Imperial Boulevard in West New York. Engine 3 was a double house that also contained Truck 2. Engine 3's radio call number was 663 and Truck 2 was 669. The station now houses Squad 6 under NHRFR and contains a Telequirt apparatus. It is the western most station in the NHRFR.

Engine 4 of the NBFD was located at 75th Street and Hudson Avenue and now houses Engine 13 under NHRFR. This is the location of the northern most Engine Company in the North Hudson region. The old station was condemned and torn down in the late 1980's. During the construction of the new station, Engine 4 first rode out of Guttenberg (quarters of the current NHRFR Rescue Company) and then moved to Engine 3's quarters on Tonnelle Avenue. Ironically, at this time there was a fire right around the corner from the closed firehouse at a duplex on 75th Street. This fire occurred on October 30th, cabbage night. Former North Bergen firefighter and current FDNY firefighter Keith Nicoliello was going to a Halloween party when he responded to the fire in a gorilla costume making it a very memorable fire. Deputy Chief Frank Miller and Firefighter James Roselle proceeded to ventilate the roof, successfully saving fellow firefighter, Captain Tom Irving, side of the duplex. The new station was finally completed in 1991 at which time the Engine Company moved back to protect this area of the city. It is still debated to this day whether or not the spirit of deceased Firefighter Charlie Noble made the transformation to the new station. North Bergen Engine 4's call number was 664.

Engine 5 was located under Town Hall at 43rd Street and Kennedy Boulevard. This was a double house that also at times housed Truck 2, the Emergency Truck, and even Truck 1 during its renovation. When Truck 1 was moved to this station, the tiller cover had to be removed so that the apparatus could fit into the firehouse. When leaving quarters, the tiller man had to duck to keep from hitting the apparatus door. There is no longer a fire station at the North Bergen Town Hall. This area of the building has been remodeled into a meeting room. The radio call number for Engine 5 was 665.

Truck 1 at 83rd Street and Kennedy Boulevard is now known as Ladder 5 under NHRFR. This is the northern most station in all of North Hudson. In 1988, a 3 foot wide hole developed in the apparatus floor of this firehouse. A major renovation had to be performed so that the floor could support the weight of the Hook and Ladder. Truck 1 of the former North Bergen Fire Department used radio call number 668.

Family Connection

A complete list of every member appointed to the North Bergen Fire Department was obtained through the records by former North Bergen Fire Department Secretary and current NHRFR employee Linda DiPaolo. It starts with the original paid members in 1924 and continues until Kevin Jackson was hired as the last North Bergen Fire Department member on May 29, 1998.

As you look through the list, you begin to see the recurrence of last names over the years. For example, Herman Gutjahr, better known as "Quackie", was hired on March 1, 1927. Years later, his son John Gutjahr was hired on June 20, 1963. More and more family members began to tell their sons, daughters, brothers, in-laws, cousins, etc. to "just take the test." Surnames such as; Andes, Affuso, Barth, Becker, Bergman, Boele, Casey, DeLeo, DeOrio, DiVincent, Donnarumma, Dvorak, Falco, Fischer, Franke, Gallagher, Gazzillo, Holling, Lang, Leahy, Lehnes, Lurig, Martin, Montagne, Murphy, Nacca, Postorino, Rausch, Rush, Smith, Stahl, Stankard, Steinel, Steiner, Sullivan, Teta, Thomas, Turner, Vasta, Viscardo, Wernli, Williams, and Zahn are repeated in the list of firefighters that were on the job. The North Bergen Fire Department also had many other relatives that did not share the same last name.

Over the years there have been numerous multi-generation firefighters. There have been four generations of Charles Thomas' on the job dating back to the volunteer Department. Current NHRFR Director, Michael DeOrio, saw his son Daniel become a third generation firefighter when he was hired by the NHRFR, and there have been numerous 2nd generation firefighters. The Montagne family had two sets of 2nd generation firefighters with Deputy Chief Frank Montagne following in his father, Captain Frank "Fish" Montagne's footsteps and Captain John Montagne and his father, Captain Bob Montagne, who happened to be the unofficial department photographer.

This family tradition continues today within the NHRFR department with such names as; Cospito, Cowan, D'Antonio, Velez and others.

The fire service sees itself as being an extended family where we are all "brothers." Over the years, several people were welcomed into this extended fire department family. For example, Reverend Wilcomes, the former fire department Chaplin, would often visit and have coffee with the men while offering words of encouragement. Later, Father Hamel, of Our Lady of Fatima Church, would often visit different stations and eventually joined the fire department basketball team. Mr. James O'Brien, owner of Weller's candy store, would visit the firehouse, often bringing a refreshment to the on duty firefighters. Mr. and Mrs. Damato would often feed the on duty firefighters when old Engine 3 was next door to their house. And who could ever forget "Aunt Susie" Romano, Dan Viscardo Sr.'s sister, making her famous pizza for various fire department events. To these and other friends of the fire department, we offer our sincere thank you.

Firehouse Life

When one looks back on their career in the North Bergen Fire Department, one can't help but remember various people and activities that occurred around the firehouse. For example, most have vivid memories of Vic Carpenter coming to the station selling his candy and clothing while exclaiming "if you don't have the money, put it on the arm."

There were many stories of the legendary Firefighter Thomas "Tacky" Gaynor. He was known for being extremely strong and for being a bit of an inventor. Tacky worked at the fire department repair shop for many years along with firefighter Frank Dvorak. Other firefighters known for their tremendous strength were Walter Barkus, who would throw a roll of hose clear over a fire engine, and Al Cody, who would make you wince in pain when shaking your hand.

Truck 2 and Engine 5 were located in a firehouse below the town hall on 43rd Street.

The shops converted a former ambulance into a field communication unit.

Many of the Officers of the department were known for their exceptional ability to train the younger firefighters. Battalion Chief Robert Supel was known as a tremendous trainer in donning the hazardous material protective equipment. Battalion Chief Doug Garrity and Captain Tommy Smith were well known for their knowledge on ropes and knots.

Some firefighters, like Captain Jack Whelan and Captain Larry Westphal, were so enthusiastic that they would arrive a day early for their shift. Other firefighters took their skills to the FDNY when they switched to the largest department in the country. Besides the aforementioned Firefighter Nicoliello, there was also Firefighters Barbanera, McMonegal, Menzel and Moran.

If you ever needed any supplies around the firehouse, you knew you could call on Captain Albie Santinello. Before him there was Captain Bernie Dvorak, Captain Otto Aimone, and Firefighter Wilbur Reck.

Several of the former members were well known as tremendous chefs. There was Curtis Smith who would make enough food to feed several crews. Firefighter Tony Affuso would cook meals using recipes from his Uncle's restaurant, Affuso's Dugout. BC Larry Westphal, DC Dennis Schack, and Firefighter Auggie Lavino were also known to have some fantastic recipes. Firefighter Frankie "Pots" Ruggiero got his nickname while cooking one of his firehouse meals. Captain Tony Avello was known for his baking as well as cooking. Firefighter George Franke Jr. would bring in various specials from his diner. The crew of Engine 4 on the 1st Platoon was known for their health food menu of vegetarian chili and sprouts.

In the old days, firefighters would pass the down time playing cards. Over the years this changed to other activities. Ping-Pong became a very popular pass-time. The matches at Truck 1 reached legendary stature at their basement ping-pong table. Some of the members known for their extraordinary ping-pong playing were Captain Tom Torre, DC Gene Romer, DC Frank Montagne and Firefighter James Roselle. Firefighter Andy Becker was known for his imitations. If he didn't become a firefighter, Andy could have earned a living as a stand-up comic.

Apparatus

There were a variety of apparatus used through the history of the North Bergen Fire Department. There are pictures of some of this equipment dating back to horse pulled apparatus.

The department used equipment made from a variety of manufacturers including; American LaFrance, Mack, Maxim, Grumman, Howe, Pierce, etc. There was also a variety of specialized equipment such as an emergency truck that had a utility ladder attached, a haz-mat truck that was eventually turned into a lighttruck. A step-van type rescue vehicle and the MSU unit that is still in operation by the NHRFR department as Safety 1. There has also been some apparatus that was refurbished and put into use by the North Bergen Fire Department. This included a burnt fire engine that was restored, a used Pierce tiller ladder from the Pittsburgh FD, a Mack pumper purchased from the FDNY and others.

There is a picture of a 1930's era engine that still had the hard rubber tires. There is a picture of a 1941 American LaFrance truck, which was unique in its narrow cab and body as well as its 75-foot aerial ladder. In 1942 North Bergen purchased a Mack pumper which was put in service as Engine 1. There is a picture of this engine in front of its quarters on Kennedy Boulevard.

In the 1950's, the North Bergen Fire Department utilized three Ward LaFrance engines. There are still retired members around who remember these pumpers from when they first got on the job. There are pictures in existence of these apparatus.

The truck that went down 86th Street hill was a 1960 Maxim ladder. North Bergen also had an open cab Maxim pumper which

North Bergen Fire Department 1924-1999

was in service at Engine 4. This was the last of the open cab apparatus to be used by the department and was still in service as a spare engine as late as 1988.

Around 1980, three Howe pumpers were put in service by the North Bergen Fire Department. These engines were originally painted white over lime green but were later repainted red. Under the direction of Chief DiStefano, these engines were specially built with a stronger transmission for the hills and with a shorter wheel base for the tight streets.

In 1986, the North Bergen Fire Department put into service a Maxim 100-foot tiller ladder truck. This apparatus was specially built to fit inside Truck 1's quarters. This apparatus was finally retired by the NHRFR in the early 2000's.

Around 1988, two Grumman telesquirts were received into the North Bergen Fire Department. Engine 2 Squirt was placed downtown in case a quick aerial operation was needed before Truck 1 was able to arrive from their uptown location. This apparatus in now Engine 11 under the NHRFR and is at the station in West New York at 66th and Jackson. Engine 3's Squirt had a built in foam tank and is currently Squad 7 in the NHRFR, located at Headquarters in West New York.

Then in the 1990's North Bergen put into service three Pierce Engines. These pumpers are still in service today and are stationed at NHRFR Engines 1, 9 and 13 respectively. These were the last apparatus to be purchased by the North Bergen Fire Department prior to the regionalization of the department.

Incidents

Over the years, the former North Bergen Fire Department has had its share of large scale incidents. These responses included various types of fire and rescues. Some of the types of fires included; high-rise fires, huge meadowland fires visible for miles, long duration pier fires, railroad fires, residential and commercial building fires and more. Some of the rescue situation included; vehicular crashes with extrication of victims, cliff rescues, water rescues, railroad crashes, industrial accidents, etc. Throughout it all, the members of the North Bergen Fire Department responded with bravery and professionalism.

The North Bergen Fire Department responded to some incidents involving aviation over the years. In foggy, misty weather, on November 8, 1956, a plane crashed into the WOR-TV tower located behind the old Embassy Theatre between 72nd Street and 73rd Street just off Bergenline Avenue. The TV tower reached 810 feet into the sky and could be seen for miles during its existence. After hitting the tower, the plane crashed into an apartment building on Hudson Avenue killing a woman resident. This incident made national news and resulted in the tower being dismantled.

Then in 1982, two airplanes collided over James J. Braddock Hudson County Park. The call came into the North Bergen Fire Department. Although the planes crashed down in Cliffside Park and Fairview, Engine 4 responded in and had one of the first lines on the resulting fire. While responding, Truck 1 ran over some debris in the road, which wound up being a wing of one of the planes.

On May 5, 1994, another aviation accident struck in North Bergen when a helicopter hit high voltage lines and crashed in the fast lane of Route 495. Although two people died aboard the helicopter, it was very fortunate that no vehicles were struck on the busy highway. The live electrical wire did however start numerous vehicle fires within the Park and Ride lot located adjacent to the highway.

Although aviation crashes are a rare incident to hit a community, this happened for a fourth time in North Bergen when a small single engine Cessna crashed on River Road on February 25th, 1995. This incident had a happy ending however when the two plane occupants were able to walk away from the crash and actually walked into the Palisade Medical center just across the street from where the plane crashed.

The trend continued with the NHRFR when the US Airways plane crashed into the Hudson River in what would become to be known as the *Miracle on the Hudson* incident.

The steep hills of North Bergen have been the backdrop to some serious and unique incidents. North Bergen is a city with the second most hills per square mile second to San Francisco. In the 1970's, Truck 1 was responding down 86th Street hill, being driven by Firefighter Harry Stahl, when the apparatus lost its brakes. The crew tried to stop the vehicle by hitting parked cars,

Reserve Engine 6, a 1975 Mack/1987 C.E.T. Refurb (Ex. F.D.N.Y.) and Engine 5's 1980 PEMFAB/Howe Pumper.

however, the momentum carried the truck through the intersection of Tonnelle Avenue. A passing vehicle broadsided the truck. The truck ended up on the west side of Tonnelle Avenue heading in a south direction. Firefighter Hank Boele had to climb down a tree to escape the tiller seat. The force of the accident caused Captain DeLeo's helmet to be damaged with a sizable piece dislodged. Luckily, all parties escaped the incident with only minor injuries.

Also, in the 1970's a fire on 80th Street hill occurred requiring the call for Mutual Aid. A West New York pumper responded and the driver had to stay inside the vehicle during the fire because the brakes would not hold the vehicle still.

During a fire on 10th Street hill, the Engine 3's air brakes gave way and the wheel chock exploded causing the apparatus to roll down hill. The chauffeur, Firefighter Dave Velez ran after the rig, jumped in and stopped the vehicle before hitting any parked vehicles. This resulted in the department purchasing new, larger wheel chocks.

The former North Bergen Fire Department has had its share of tragedy, heartbreak, and close calls over the years. In 1952, Lt. William Guth was killed in the line of duty when he fell from the Hook and Ladder Truck while responding to a fire. In 1938, Firefighter Chauncey Hamlin died in a car accident responding to a fire in his personal vehicle. Former North Bergen Firefighter Vincent Neglia was killed in the line of duty in 2006 fighting a fire in Union City as part of the NHRFR.

Firefighter Robert Magnuson suffered a serious eye injury when a large hose gave way at a downtown fire. Firefighter David Velez was seriously injured during a mutual aid fire in Union City, when he fell from a ladder while rescuing and protecting an unhurt child. He subsequently retired from the NHRFR department. Firefighters Rich Gallagher and Steve McGauley were injured at a fire on Paterson Plank Road when they fell through a hole in the floor. Captain Donald Williamson was injured fighting an intense wind fueled fire in an apartment building on 17th Street and Kennedy Boulevard.

In 1980, at the Columbia Park Bowling Alley fire, BC Charlie Severino nearly fell through the weakened roof. He was in up to his armpits when he was removed by Captain Tom Irving. In the early 1990's, at a fire near 75th Street and Broadway, Captain Mike Motta nearly fell off an icy roof when he was rescued by DC Nick Gazzillo.

The North Bergen Fire Department had its share of high-rise fires over the years. A fire at the Westview Towers resulted in the loss of four lives when an oxygen tank exploded inside an apartment. Firefighter Ed Quinn performed a daring rescue attempt injuring his shoulder. At one of the several Stonehenge fires, now Captain Tim Steinel was briefly trapped in a smoke filled elevator narrowly escaping tragedy.

On October 26, 1992, there was a fire at the Orchard Grove Tavern on 95th Street. The entire building was destroyed, except for a small area of the building where five life size religious figures were untouched. Deputy Chief Montagne, Captain Butch Ditursi, and Captain Nick Pallotta witnessed the statues move across the floor. Members of the Italian-American Society called it "divine intervention" in explaining the saving of the valuable religious icons.

National Cylinder, on 84th Street and Tonnelle Avenue was the scene of a fatal fire where acetylene tanks exploded into the air. Then on June 14, 1992, several propane tanks exploded at a spectacular fire at Alexander's Pallets off of Paterson Plank Road, by the meadowlands.

In the 1970's, a huge church fire occurred at Grove Church on 46th Street and Kennedy Boulevard. This fire was fought under the command of Deputy Chief James Hargaden.

On February 3, 1985, during frigid cold weather the Davis Grande warehouse caught fire. This commercial building was located at 4401 Dell Avenue. This fire was a prolonged operation were many of the hose-lines were frozen solid and was fought under the command of DC Howie DeSavino.

Another fire that could be seen from as far away as New York was the fire at the unfinished Columbia Park condo complex located at 31st Street and Kennedy Boulevard, on June 26, 1994.

Miller's Slaughter House, on 5th Street and Tonnelle Avenue was the scene of many General Alarm fires. These fires would involve various sections of the large building over the years, as well as long duration fires deep seated within the pig manure.

There were some tremendous rescues performed such as the one by Captain Joe DiVincent and his crew at an apartment building fire at 85th Street and Kennedy Boulevard where a ladder rescue was performed removing the nephew of Firefighter Donald Rush. Captain Al Santoniello performed the heroic rescue of a wheelchair bound woman at an apartment building on 79th Street and Kennedy Boulevard.

On April 8, 1997, in a prelude to regionalization, Engine 662 responded on a mutual aid fire to 609 Central Avenue in Union City. At this scene Firefighters Brian Canetti, Tom Steinel and Al Cody performed a dramatic ladder rescue.

On October 6, 1998, off duty Firefighter Mike Fischer rescued an elderly neighbor at what would turn out to be a three alarm fire.

These were just a small list of some the various incidents and rescues that the North Bergen Fire Department responded to over the years. The bravery and determination of the responders lives on today with the NHRFR department.

Activities

Over the years, members of the North Bergen Fire Department participated in a number of outside activities, some of which are still going on to this day. In the 1980's, a tradition began started by Firefighter George Welch and Captain James Lemke. Welch and Lemke wanted to brighten the spirits of those children who were unfortunate enough to be in the hospital during the Christmas Holiday season. Under their guidance, members of the department chip in money to buy toys for the children. Firefighters, friends and family would wrap those gifts at the annual Holiday gift-wrapping party. Then, teams of volunteers distribute the gifts to children in the area hospitals. Other members such as Firefighter Dave Velez, Captain Scott Marione and Captain Kirk Miick have been instrumental in keeping this tradition going strong, still today under the NHRFR department.

The North Bergen Fire Department traditionally ran a family picnic. Retired members talked about the picnic taking place at locations in North Bergen including Orchard Grove's Buonocomino Park and at the grounds of the former Lincoln Inn. Later the picnic moved out to Cook's Lake so that attendees could swim in the lake. Recently, Captain Kirk Miick had the picnic moved to picnic grounds in Sayreville, New Jersey. There are fond memories of retired firefighter Dan Viscardo Sr. leading the wet towel game and the legendary egg toss. Recently, those events were replaced with the horseshoe contest and the blow-up jumping station for the children. There was always an annual softball game between the "young guys and the "old guys." Danny Viscardo Sr. was always the umpire and his son was always on the young guys team. When Firefighter and past union president Patrick Keenan would throw a perfect pitch to apparently strike out Dan Viscardo Jr., his father would always hesitate in calling strike three.

Members of the department often participated in various sporting events. There was often a fire department softball team staffed by such members as; Deputy Chief Vincent "Buddy" Conroy, DC Guy DiVincent, DC Frank Miller, DC Gene Romer, Captain Steve Floriani, Captain Joe Lavelle, Captain Dom Rovito, Captain Kevin Riley, Firefighter Nick Vasta, FF Patty Nacca, FF Donald "Red" Holling, FF James Murphy, Captain Willy Shopmann, and many others. There was a yearly charity basketball and football game played against the police department. The quarterback of the football game was often Firefighter Don Marino or Battalion Chief David Donnarumma.

North Bergen Fire Department 1924-1999

Over the years, many of the departments' members worked in Fire Prevention and would visit the local schools to teach the children about fire safety. Some of these members included; Deputy Chief Rudy Cellini, Battalion Chief Charles Severino, Captain Tom Irving, Captain Joe Zavardino, Captain John "Butch" Ditursi, Captain Brian Boele, Firefighter Gary Ippolito, Firefighter Anthony Racioppi, Firefighter Glenn Turner and others.

Many of the members became active in the union over the years. Some of the past union presidents were; Theodore DiGiammo, John Bielka, George Noe, Frankie Becker, George Affuso, Patrick Keenan, Don Marino, and Deputy Chief Dave Leahy. Besides negotiating contracts and tending to labor issues, union officials often participated in charitable events such as the traditional fishing contest held at Hudson County Park. One fondly remembers Mike "Big Bird" Fischer cooking hot dogs for the children during these events.

Various members would get involved in the Relief Association over the years. Some of these members were Captain Frank Vasta Sr., BC Frank Vasta Jr., FF Iggy Pizzo, Captain Ralph Vanore, Captain Ron Zampella, FF Patrick Keenan, FF Thomas Schwartz and others.

A tradition that has been occurring for generations within the North Bergen Fire Department is the decoration of deceased members graves with American flags. Each year, around the time of Memorial Day, the grave decorating committee will visit the graves of deceased members buried in all of the six North Bergen cemeteries as well as the Faiview Cemetery and Madonna Cemetery in Fort Lee. Former committee members included Captain Mike Falco Sr., DC James Hargaden, Firefighter Al Pantaleo, Herman Gutjahr, Andy Eller, Edward Ebel and others. Current members are DC Charles Thomas, Sr., BC Charles Thomas Jr., FF Stefan Vassallo and NHRFR FF Kevin Cowan. There is an open invitation for the other former fire departments of North Hudson to include their deceased members in this remembrance.

Members of the former department still meet for periodic luncheons. Dan Viscardo Sr. was instrumental in starting the tradition. Captain Ron Zampella, BC Al Santoniello and FF Patrick Keenan now lead the tradition. These luncheons have changed locations over the years and currently occur at DePalma's Restaurant in North Bergen. This event has been growing to include other members of the NHRFR department.

There was an annual charitable golf outing which was headed by BC Marc Johnson and FF Glen Turner.

These and other events, activities and notices can be viewed on the web at www.yahoo.com/group/northbergenfirefighters. You will have to join the group to have access to this site.

Best Wishes

It is our sincere hope that this yearbook brings back many fond memories of events of the past. We extend our apologies for any errors or omissions associated with this historical account. The members of the former North Bergen Fire Department acted with bravery and professionalism in the performance of their duties. There were many other rescues and events that took place but due to space constraints are not listed here. To those members involved we offer our gratitude and admiration. We wish you and your family all of the best and a happy and healthy future. ("North Bergen Fire Department 1924-1999" history submitted by Battalion Chief Charles Thomas)

Engine 4's 1980 Pemfab/Howe 1250 GPM pumper.

North Bergen Fire Department 1924-1999

Union City Fire Department 1925-1999

The City of Union City was formed as a consolidation of two bordering towns in the mid-1920s when several North Hudson municipalities placed the question of merging to the voters. The other towns rejected the merge into a bigger North Hudson city. You might say that a seed for regional projects started here. In addition, the residents of former West Hoboken were instrumental in preserving North Hudson's separate municipalities in 1869.

Union City is the result of a consolidation of the Town of West Hoboken and the Town of Union (also known as Union Hill). West Hoboken was incorporated in 1861 into a township. In 1884 it became the Town of West Hoboken with a population of 3000. Union Hill became incorporated as the Town of Union in 1861 with a population of 600. This locality benefited by the migration of people from New York who found it convenient to get to, was pleasant, and they established homes here. Union Hill's Bergenline Avenue rapidly became the shopping center for all of the surrounding towns.

The consolidation of West Hoboken and Union Hill took placed at a referendum held on March 4, 1924, and the name Union City was adopted on June 1, 1925. The 1.3 square-mile city boast a population of over 65,000.

Now, it might be interesting to note how North Hudson remained North Hudson.

According to a West Hoboken history book, in 1868, "a grand scheme" originated in Jersey City whereby a bill was prepared and introduced in the Legislature, which provided for the holding of an election in Hudson County, at which voters were to determine whether or not the county would be consolidated into one city and under the corporate name of Jersey City. "The latter city being deep into debt had her eyes on the rest of the county as a fertile field for reaping new taxes and so help reduce her debt."

The bill passed the Legislature and the election took place on October 5, 1869, and had it not been for the citizens of West Hoboken, the desires of Jersey City would have been gratified.

Previous to the passing of the bill, mass meetings were held in West Hoboken, under the auspices of the Township Committee, and the citizens, to protest against its passing, or in the event of its

1936 Emergency Squad

passage, to arouse the voters to a sense of their duty in opposing its adoption at the election which followed.

This agitation bore good fruit, for when the result of the election was made known, it was seen that all the southern end of the county, as well as the northern end, excepting West Hoboken

Union City Fire Department 1925-1999

Rescue 1's 1948 Ford.

Union City Fire Department's 1965 Pierce 85-ft Pitman Snorkel.

Truck 3's 1938 American LaFrance straight-frame aerial ladder.

and Bayonne, voted in favor. The vote in West Hoboken stood 95 for and 256 against. By this action, North Hudson was forced to stay out, thereby keeping Jersey City below Paterson Plank Road.

The Town of Union had a volunteer fire department consisting of two engine companies, two hose companies and two hook & ladder companies at the time of consolidation. West Hoboken had a paid department. Previous to that, a 1912 W.H.F.D. program listed a volunteer department consisting of seven companies with 12 pieces of apparatus.

West Hoboken's career department's union was the Firemen's Mutual Benevolent Association (FMBA) Local 12. That local later became the U.C.F.D. union. According to a copy of Local 12's First Annual Ball Program from 1922, the career W.H.F.D.'s union listed the following members: 1 Chief, 1 Assistant Chief, 4 Captains, 4 Lieutenants and 48 Firemen. The program provided photos of three engine companies and two hook & ladder companies.

Excerpts from "An ordinance to establish, maintain, regulate and control a Fire Department," which commenced on January 1, 1926, included:

Section 6. "On and after the first day of January, 1926, the Fire Department of the City shall consist of the following superior officers and firemen, namely: One Chief, One Assistant Chief, Twenty Captains, Ninety Firemen."

The career West Hoboken firemen became members of the U.C.F.D., and, "The Commissioner of the Fire Department shall merely appoint additional new men to bring the total membership of the Department to the total fixed by this ordinance."

Section 17. "...the Fire Department divided into two bodies or platoons, which shall be designated as a day force and a night force, and said day force and night force shall alternate on tours of duty every fourth day. The hours of duty of the day force shall be from eight o'clock A.M. to six o'clock P.M., and

Rescue 1's 1964 GMC/H&H apparatus.

Chief Edward A. Beadle (fourth from left) with officers and members after the new rescue truck was delivered in 1964 at the 16th Street firehouse.

36 **Union City Fire Department 1925-1999**

the hours of the night force shall be from six o'clock P.M. to eight o'clock the following morning; provided that on every fourth day, and vice versa, the number of hours on duty herein fixed may be exceeded, but one force shall be at liberty at all times; excepting that in case of serious conflagration..."

Section 20. "The pay or compensation to be allowed or paid to members of the Fire Department shall be as follows: a. Chief-$3,100 per annum; b. Assistant Chief-$2,900 per annum; c. Captain-$2,400 per annum; d. Fireman as follows: $1,700 per annum for the first year of service...$2,100 per annum for the fifth year of service and thereafter."

The salaries of the members of the W.H.F.D. "continued to be based upon the years of service heretofore rendered by them to the Town of West Hoboken."

Old U.C.F.D. running cards showed a three-alarm assignment consisting of six engine companies, one chemical wagon, three truck companies and an emergency squad.

In a post World Ward II report on Union City, it listed the Fire Department as running six engine companies, three truck companies and an emergency squad, "most of which is of modern design, and has latest proven equipment." The report showed the Fire Department employing 114 men, of which 24 were officers.

Over the years fire apparatus in the department consisted mostly units manufactured by American LaFrance (ALF), Seagrave and Mack. The apparatus color was red; however, during the late 1930's white was the fad that many area departments jumped on including Union City. In later years some of these rigs were re-painted red.

The Union City Fire Department (U.C.F.D.) had some apparatus firsts. For example, in 1938 the department received the first ALF aerial ladder with a hydraulic hoist, and it was the only ALF ever built with a three-section wood aerial ladder. The ALF 400 Series model was painted white. Also in 1938, the U.C.F.D. received the very first cab-forward-design ALF JQ Deluxe 85-foot service aerial, in white. Firemen did not like this straight-frame design and its poor maneuverability compared to the tiller aerial units.

Over the years Union City's apparatus received write-ups in national fire service publications. A 1936 issue of "Fire Engineering" magazine bore an article on an "Emergency Flood Light Truck of Progressive Design Recently Put In Service by Union City, New Jersey, Department of Public Safety."

The flood light unit evolved into an emergency squad and then a rescue unit. In 1964 the department received a $33,500 GMC tilt-cab rescue truck with rescue body built by H&H Truck & Tank Company of Jersey City. This rig had a 300-horsepower, 12-cylinder GMC engine and enclosed rear cabin. Rescue 1 had four oxygen outlets with masks for reviving either firemen or residents when overcome by smoke. Mounted on the rear deck were six 500-watt spotlights fed by two removable 7- kW generators.

This apparatus was featured in magazine articles and described its 900-feet of cable on reels to put the power where needed. A 1964 fire magazine described it as a "Satellite Cable Reel System an Innovation in Union City, New Jersey"

This rescue truck was later sold to the Mahwah Fire Department. In the 1980's it was acquired by NBC Productions and was transformed into a police emergency looking truck by Saulsbury Fire Apparatus of Tully, New York, for a short lived TV show called "True Blue." The outside of the truck was made to look like an NYPD ESU truck with blue and white colors and police lettering. The truck was later acquired by a company in Brooklyn that leases vehicles to movie and TV productions. This rig can be seen in the background of "crime scenes" on shows such as "NYPD Blue" and "Law and Order." The paint on this truck has been changed to all white with current NYPD graphics and is still in use.

In 1965 the UCFD placed into service the first "Snorkel" articulating platform device in Hudson County. The 85-foot Pitman, mounted an FWD chassis, was assigned to 16th Street and known as Snorkel 1. It operated at many major fires in North Hudson and Jersey City. In 1966 the UCFD placed into service the first diesel powered pumper in the county. This FWD rig had a 336-horsepower diesel motor and automatic transmission. It had a 1250 gpm pump and could deliver high pressure fog at 600 pounds per square inch.

In 1969 Engine Company 1 received a Seagrave pumper with a 1500 gpm pump-one of the largest capacity pumps in the area at the time. It also had high pressure fog capability. A second Snorkel was also delivered to the city in 1970. This was a 75-foot model built on a Seagrave chassis and diesel powered. It was designated Snorkel 3, for Truck 3, but never served that company. It was determined that the floor at the 43rd Street firehouse would not support the rig and it was assigned to 29th Street. History repeated itself, as firemen were not happy with the maneuverability of the Snorkels. Snorkel 3 has a longer chassis and was sold to East Brunswick Independent Fire Company 2 where it is painted that

Engine 5, Battalion Chief and Truck 2 at the 29th Street Firehouse in the early 1960s.

Truck 3 and Engine 4 at the 43rd Street Firehouse in the early 1960s.

Union City Fire Department 1925-1999 37

Truck 3 operating on Kennedy Boulevard near Seventh Street.

company's white color and still serves. The money received from this sale went to the purchased of a 1973 Seagrave 100-foot tiller that is currently North Hudson Reserve Ladder 6.

The first 4-door enclosed cab pumpers went into service in 1989 with the delivery of two Mack/Ward 79 1500 gpm pumpers for Engines 1 and 5.

Union City has had its share of major fires. On May 31, 1934, a five-hour fire at St. Michael's Monastery Church left only the granite walls standing. Firemen were hampered by insufficient water pressure to reach flames consuming the 190-foot-high dome. This fire became one of the most notable that Jersey City's American LaFrance 65-foot tractor drawn water tower operated at. When the fire was out, Rev. Edward Groggins issued an immediate statement, "We will rebuild at once." By November, services were being held in the reconstructed church basement. On September 29, 1936, St. Michael's Monastery was rededicated.

Chief George C. Friedel was caught in an explosion at a commercial building on July 16, 1935, and was severely injured. He had 14 hospitalizations over the years to correct damage to his spinal cord and died from those injuries in 1962 at age 59. He was appointed Chief of Department in 1931 and gave up that position to Deputy Chief Barney Korn in 1958 when he could no longer carry out his duties. At that time he held a longevity state record as fire chief.

Records are not complete, but in the late 1930's or early 1940's a city fireman was killed while operating at a smokey fire that started in the basement of Thomas Photography Studio, 3510 Bergenline Avenue. Over 40 firemen required medical attention and 16 were hospitalized.

On January 10, 1959, Captain Charles Royce, a veteran of 24-years on the job, had just emerged from a smoke-filled cellar of Summit Pizza, on Summit Avenue, when he keeled over on the sidewalk, according to a "Hudson Dispatch" article. Dr. Tardio, of North Hudson Hospital, attributed death to coronary thrombosis.

In January, 1966, seven people died in a furnished apartment house fire on 48th Street. It was described as the worst fire disaster in the history of the city at that time.

While Weehawken Fireman Frank Nagurka was working at a fire at 108-48th Street, Union City, in March, 1970, he was looking for a roof hatch to open for ventilation purposes. He fell nearly 40-feet down an inside air shaft to a basement level enclosed court yard between two apartment buildings. Although in intense pain, Nagurka called out to his brother firemen on the roof to warn them of the unprotected air shaft. After rehabilitation, Nagurka returned to duty and retired with the rank of deputy chief.

On July 9, 1970, a general alarm fire at a corner apartment house at 553-41st Street, at Kennedy Boulevard, took the lives of Fireman John Promersperger and three members of the Chinea family. As flames consumed the upper floors, the wall on the 41st Street side wavered and then collapsed. Then the Kennedy Boulevard wall, with firemen working on the fire escape, collapsed carrying those men to the ground into a pile of rubble. Injured were Chief Edward A. Beadle, Captain Frank Crandal, and Firemen Robert Cervate, Roger Estabrook, Robert Michelin, Anthony Novembre and George Bolte.

Deputy Chief John Provede died on January 2, 1973, of a severe heart attack he suffered after fighting a two-alarm fire involving a 48th Street furniture store. Provede had returned to his 41st Street home after the fire was extinguished when he collapsed. Members of the young volunteer ambulance squad, Lenny Inzerillo (who later became a city firefighter) and George Drimones performed CPR and administered oxygen. A neighborhood doctor, off duty firemen and police officers were there to assist. After reviving the chief several times, as oxygen supplies from every emergency vehicle on

Union City Fire Department 1925-1999

the scene ran out, the EMT's performed mouth-to-mouth resuscitation on the way to North Hudson Hospital, where Provede was pronounced dead. A spokesman for the ambulance corps said D.C. Provede died, clinically speaking, nine times while being worked on by the EMT's, keeping him alive until they got to the hospital.

Fireman Robert Colavito was killed on the evening of December 12, 1977, while trying to rescue a captain who was falling through a rooftop hole. The fire involved a two-story dwelling at 3304 Pleasant Avenue, Weehawken. A bystander pulled the alarm box on the Union City side of the street. The city firemen were working on the roof to vent when Captain Philip DeVito lost his footing and began slipping into the hole. Fireman Colavito and Robert Michelin were standing close to the edge and tried to grab him, but they were thrown off balance by the heat and flames shooting off of the vented hole and slipped off the ice-slicked roof. Colavito landed on his head and was killed. Fireman Michelin suffered extensive leg injuries. Fireman Colavito had two brothers on the U.C.F.D. at the timer of his death – Joseph and Thomas. Raymond Colavito, the son of Thomas, later joined the U.C.F.D. and is now part of the regional department. Captain DeVito was saved by other fireman and not seriously hurt. After extensive rehabilitation, a determined Michelin returned to work as the city fire official. His son, Glen, joined the U.C.F.D. and is currently a member of the regional department.

A seed was planted for a regional fire department in 1982 when the North Hudson Fire Communications Center was open at 4911 Broadway, West New York. This became the dispatch center for Union City, West New York, North Bergen, Weehawken, and later Guttenberg.

According to an article in the February 22, 1982, edition of "The Jersey Journal," "Some years ago, a Stevens Institute team recommended that the (North Hudson) mayor's council consolidate fire departments, merging certain firehouses as a step toward that goal. But the council elected to take a 'go slow' approach and went for the joint fire communications set up."

The new Fire Control was quickly broken in by the U.C.F.D. Only hours after Fire Control took over dispatching Union City fire companies, a mutual aid fire struck at the Transport of NJ (now NJ Transit) bus garage, known locally as "the car barns," on the evening of May 22, 1982. Some 75 firefighters responded to the 29th Street fire where 13 buses and the building were damaged.

The U.C.F.D. became one of the first departments in the area to adopt a 24 hour on-72 hour off work schedule in the late 1960's. This work chart is now used by a majority of career departments in the state.

Edward A. Beadle was promoted to Chief of Department in 1961. In 1968 he was named president of the International Association of Fire Chiefs. The prestigious organization was made up of 8,700 members from all over the world.

Fireman Mario Rossi was known around the state for his FMBA work. He was Local 12's state delegate for many years and also served as president of the North Hudson Firemen's Mutual Aid Association and the local exempts association. The annual FMBA state picnic is now named in his memory. Fireman Rossi received a Bronze Award for Heroism in 1970 by the state FMBA. On January 19, 1970, he rescued a four-year-old boy during a general alarm fire at 4603 Park Avenue. The fire took the lives of a mother and child in another apartment in the building.

In the early 2000's Union City Board of Education Interim Board Secretary Anthony Dragona has a vision to save the Exempts firehouse on Palisade Avenue near 44th Street that was in a state of disrepair. The building was originally the quarters of Dispatch Hook & Ladder Company 2 of the Town of Union. Dragona had served as public safety commissioner in the 1980's. With the help of state funding, the building was renovated and turned into a fire museum for students and residents to enjoy on the second floor, and a student registration office on the ground floor (old apparatus bay).

In 1999, the U.C.F.D. had dwindled down to 94 members running four engines and two trucks, apparently in anticipation of a regional department being established.

(*"Union City Fire Department 1925-1999"* history submitted by Ron Jeffers, Department Photographer/Honorary Battalion Chief)

Former Rescue 1 is now used in movie and TV productions as a New York City Police Emergency Service Truck.

Weehawken Fire Department
1861-1999

Baldwin Hose Company, circa 1800s.

Baldwin Hose Company, circa 1900s.

Weehawken was founded on March 15, 1859; the population was under 300 people. Fire coverage for the town was from a charter that was put forth to the Senate and the General Assembly of the State of New Jersey for "An Act to Incorporate the Weehawken Fire Department" with the townships of North Bergen on February 27, 1861, and the Township of Union (West New York) on March 6, 1861. This allowed Weehawken residents to become part of the township fire department but be housed in surrounding towns. The members would have to serve the Department for seven years to achieve exempt firefighter status. Still with the charter firefighters, most fires were fought with the old bucket brigade, or just had their belongings salvaged from the fire. Any fire on the waterfront was fought with railroad tugs that were equipped with fire pumps, from Erie Railroad.

In 1883, when the Hackensack Water Tower opened in town everything changed and fire hydrants popped up everywhere. The first township Volunteer Firefighter Company opened in the downtown area as the Baldwin Hose Company 1, named after Aaron Baldwin, the President of the Weehawken Stock Yard Company, which supplied livestock for the Erie Railroad. The person picked to run the company was Simon Kelly, yardmaster for the Erie Railroad at the time; he became the first Foreman (Chief) of the Company. Kelly would later become the Chief of Police and Mayor of Weehawken from 1885 to 1896, only missing 1890. The building for the fire company was an old two story wood frame building on the Boulevard, north of 19th Street. Housing two bays, the first piece of fire apparatus obtained for the town was a second hand, hand drawn hose cart from Newburgh, New

Weehawken Fire Department 1861-1999

Highwood Fire Company

Weehawken Fire Department 1861-1999

York called "Old Hickory", probably after the ex-President Andrew Jackson. In a fire situation, the nearest hydrant to the fire would be wrapped with the cart hose, and moved to the fire. Enough hose would be pulled off to fight the fire, and a nozzle would be added. Hydrant pressure was around 40 pounds, but in the event of a fire, the Hackensack Water Company would up the pressure to 60 pounds.

The next section of the town that became populated was the Heights section of town, and on December 7, 1896, Palisades Hose Company 2 opened, today it is Safety 1, which runs out of Jane Street. Housed in this fire house was a hose wagon, which was a wagon with its bed, loaded with hose, ladders and hand tools were mounted. This wagon was drawn by two horses. The town did not keep horses for the fire department, so when the fire bells sounded, the town people would volunteer their horse teams for the cause. In 1897, a third firehouse opened at 49th Street and Boulevard East called Clifton Hose Company 3, and in 1900, Highwood Hose Company 4 opened.

In 1898, the firehouses had metal frame towers erected next to them with special ordered bells. Today the Highwood Fire bell that was made in 1907 can be found on Boulevard East at Hamilton Park. Before this, old railroad wheel rims were mounted outside a firehouse for alarms or were summed by church bells. Also in the same year, the Gamewell Fire Alarm Company installed fire alarm boxes around town. By 1912, the age of the motorized pumper appeared when the township bought a KNOX Engine. These units needed engineers to operate the new rigs, and this led to the first paid firefighters, since qualified personnel were needed to run the machinery. The first motorized aerial was a Christy Front Wheel Drive, and by 1919, the whole department was motorized.

Clifton Hose Company, Weehawken, New Jersey, in the early 1900s.

On June 2, 1926, the ordinance passed for a full time paid department, the first paid Chief was William O'Neil, and he was Chief from 1926 to 1951. Chief O'Neil was known for being a fire department innovator with the importance of navy nozzles and the ability to go into a fog stream, to one of the first 100-foot aerial trucks in the North Hudson county area when the town bought a 1941 American La France truck.

For the 73 years that the paid department existed, the town had five full chiefs ending with Chief Cahill in the 1980s. The last two "Chief of Operations" were only the rank of Deputy Chief, and ended with the formation of the North Hudson Regional Fire and Rescue on January 11, 1999.

(*"Weehawken Fire Department 1861-1999" history submitted by Captain William Demontreux.*)

Engine 2, circa 1924.

Weehawken Fire Department 1861-1999

Guttenberg Fire Department 1873-1999

The Guttenberg Fire Department grew out of the Home Guard, formed in the Civil War days to protect the community from occasional invasions by "roughnecks" from New York City. Members of the Home Guard organized Washington Hook & Ladder Company #2, of what was then called the Weehawken Fire Department on July 15, 1863. The company was organized in Joseph Schwartzmeier's Hotel, which stood on Franklin Avenue, between Bull's Ferry Road and First Street.

The headquarters was established in a one-story building on the south side of Franklin Avenue, just west of Bull's Ferry Road, which came known as the Truck House. When the Town Hall was completed in 1890, the company moved there and has remained there since. In 1873, the company changed its name to Washington Hook & Ladder Company #1 of Guttenberg.

The first equipment purchased by the Department, paid for by entertainments and popular subscriptions, was delivered on February 22, 1864, and remained in service forty-seven years. Manufactured in New York, it was brought to Guttenberg by way of the Canal Street Ferry under the escort of the Volunteer Empire Hook & Ladder Company #8 of New York City.

The first Officers of the Fire Department were Joseph Schwartzmeier, Foreman; Frank Gerard, Assistant Foreman; Mathias Klein, Secretary; and Adolph Meckert, Treasurer.

The formation of the present Washington Hose Company dates from July 27, 1881, when a meeting to discuss the organization of a chemical company was held in the old truck house. The company was incorporated August 8, 1881, and on September 5, the following officers were elected: F. W. Hermann, Foreman; Charles Klein, Engineer; J. E. Eits, President; J. H. Wertz, Vice President; Alfred Lurcott, Secretary; Henry J. Gorden, Treasurer; Herman Klein, Sergeant-at-Arms; and E. Umhoefer, Assistant Sergeant-at-Arms.

Eclipse Hose Company 4's 1962 Maxim 750 GPM Pumper.

Volunteer firefighters on the 1962 Maxim were known as Eclipse Hose Company 4 and the paid men were Engine Company 1.

The 1962 Maxim with the addition of a plywood "Riot Roof."

Guttenberg Fire Department 1873-1999

The company's first equipment was a soda-acid type chemical wagon, purchased from a Mr. Haywood of New York City. This was paid for in installments, the company members paying these off by individual loans to the company. The apparatus was installed with a parade from the Hoboken Ferry, in which companies from West New York, Town of Union (now Union City), New Durham, and Carlstadt took part.

The Eclipse Hose Company had its origin in the Eclipse Social Club, which met some one hundred years ago at John J. Daley's Tavern near the present Bergenline Avenue and Sixty-Eight Street. Wanting to use for some useful purpose a profit of forty dollars realized on a picnic, the club acted upon a proposal to purchase a hose carriage and organize a fire company.

On July 6, 1894, the company was organized and became known as Eclipse Hose Company #4. Frank B. Kelly and John J. Daley were appointed a committee to purchase an apparatus. They secured a Monitor Hose Carriage, which had previously seen service at Ossining, New York, for $450, on a cash payment of $100. The balance was paid off in due time through the efforts of the company members.

The first officers of the company were Frank X. Lambert, Foreman; D. Joseph Lahres, Assistant Foreman; Frank B. Kelly, Recording Secretary; Fred W. Kraemer, Financial Secretary; Joseph Schulz, Treasure; and Joseph J. Allgeier, Sergeant-at-Arms.

In connection with the fire companies, the following may be interesting. When the town hall was opened in 1890, rules were made for the building's superintendent. Section III provided that "he shall ring the Fire Bell continuously when fires are discovered East of Third Street, and when Fires are West of Third Street, he is to give two taps, turn the bell three times continuously and repeat the same successively."

In the 1930s the Town hired two paid firefighters to off set the volunteer fire department. These men worked 24 hours shifts by themselves and off 24 hours and so on. These men did all the duties of the fire service and what ever the else the town needed.

Then in 1955 the town hired a third firefighter, to give them three shifts. The men worked a 56 hour work week, 24 hours on and 48 hours off, and so on. This stayed in effect until January 1999, when North Hudson Regional Fire and Rescue took over.

The Guttenberg paid Fire Department doubled in size in January 1993 with the hiring of an additional three firefighters. With the additional firefighters, the department took on the role Medical First Responder Program. This was due to the town did not having an Ambulance Squad.

(*"Guttenberg Fire Department 1873-1999" history submitted by Captain Sean Sullivan*)

The last fully assembled piece of fire apparatus built by Mack Trucks went to Guttenberg in 1984 using a Mack MC chassis.

Washington Hose Company 2 had a 1974 American fire apparatus 1500 GPM pumper that was purchased from Elkins Park, Pennsylvania, thus the tan color.

Guttenberg Fire Department 1873-1999

County Numbering System

The regional started on January 11, 1999. The apparatus where re-lettered with new North Hudson Logo's on the door and used the old county call numbers on the apparatus.

The call numbers are as follows:

Union City Engine's 21 to 27
Union City Truck's 11 to 13
Union City Rescue 30
Weehawken Engine's 201 to 204
Weehawken Truck's 221 to 222
West New York Engine's 303 to 311
West New York Truck's 321 to 322
West New York Emergency Truck 337

Guttenberg Engine's 501 to 503
Guttenberg Truck 523
North Bergen Engine's 661 to 666
North Bergen Truck's 668 to 669
North Bergen Rescue 660

Effective May 1, 1999, the apparatus assigned numbers from south to north Engine's 1 to 14 Truck's 1 to 5.

Engine #22

Truck #13

Truck R

Engine #306

Engine #307

Engine #308

Truck #523

Truck #669

Truck #2

Squad Engine

North Hudson Regional Fire & Rescue 1999-2009

North Hudson Regional Fire & Rescue 1999-2009

Something unique for the fire service in the Northeastern part of the country was accomplished on January 11, 1999. Imagine having five different jigsaw puzzles of Noah's Ark, and dumping them into a pile, and then trying to make them into one puzzle. You will have some pieces that fit and other pieces have to be forced into place. Some are cut and molded to fit, but there are still a lot of pieces left out of this giant puzzle. When you are done and step back there is still no clear picture of this great feat that the individual puzzles possessed, but the aim of all five puzzles together is not to recreate the great flood scene of Noah and his family, but to create a new picture that has nothing to with the original five pictures. This new picture could have endless combinations. North Hudson Regional faced this dilemma.

Five Northern Hudson County, New Jersey, municipalities merged to create a regional fire department. The merge included the Fire Departments of Union City, North Bergen, West New York, Weehawken and Guttenberg. The purpose of this department includes reducing alarm response time, increase manpower on a first alarm, and in time would save taxpayers money.

North Hudson is a jigsaw puzzle of borderlines. Many firehouses are within blocks of each other in different towns. The geographically long narrow region is a contiguous urban area where it is often difficult to know when one has crossed a civic boundary. The street grid runs from 2nd Street to the south up to 91st Street to north. The Eastern border is River Road or Port Imperial Boulevard, which runs along the Hudson River waterfront, and the Western border is Westside Avenue, which runs along the Hackensack River. The total area of North Hudson is 9.4 square miles.

North Hudson is one of the most densely populated and congested, areas of the country. The new Fire Department protects approximately 250,000 residents. Fire hazards include many attached wood-frame multiple-occupancy dwellings, high rise residential structures, light and heavy industry, waterfront marinas and ferries, the Lincoln Tunnel, railroad lines, and a commuter light rail system.

It also includes one of the longest business districts in the country along Bergenline Avenue, a major commercial district in North Hudson. Even though Palisade Avenue runs continuously from 2nd Street in Union City to the George Washington Bridge in Fort Lee, Bergenline Avenue is the longest commercial avenue in the state of New Jersey having over 300 retail stores and restaurants. It is also known as the miracle mile. While it is a narrow one-way street throughout Union City, it becomes a four lane two-way street from 48th Street in Union City to 90th Street in North Bergen.

A merger of fire departments in Hudson County, located directly across the Hudson River from New York City, has been a topic of discussion by local officials since the 1960's. A study, which included all Hudson County fire departments, was made in the 1970's, but no action was taken then.

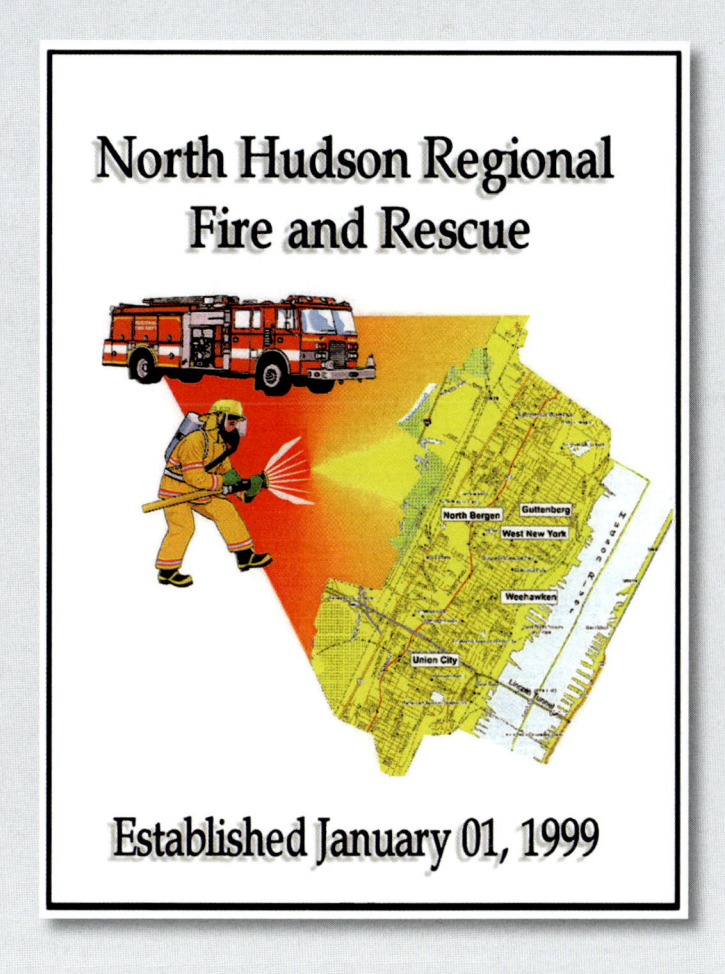

North Hudson Regional Fire and Rescue

PURPOSE
The new department will send the companies closest to a fire to that fire regardless of municipal boundaries, saving time

COVERAGE
Provides firefighting services for Union City, North Bergen, West New York, Weehawken and Guttenberg (8.6 miles, 160,000 residents)

COST
An estimated $29 million to run the new department

CONTRIBUTIONS
Union City: 33 percent
North Bergen: 26.5 percent
West New York: 25.5 percent
Weehawken: 15 percent
Guttenberg: $1.5 million

ROBERT AIELLO — Chairman of the North Hudson Regional Fire and Rescue board

ANTHONY PRESUTTI — WNY fire chief and member of NHRFR "transition group"

MICHEAL DeORIO — North Bergen deputy fire director and transition group member

JEFF WELZ — Weehawken public safety director and transition group member

ROBERT JONES — Acting Union City fire chief and transition group member

Selling the houses and equipment could net the new department $1.67 million, the consultants estimate.

With six fewer houses to maintain and less apparatus to replace, participating towns would save $450,000 a year and perhaps as much as $6.75 million over the next 20 years, they say.

Firefighter union leaders like Union City's Glen Michelin and North Bergen's Dominick Marino worry that the mayors are rushing to gut the strength of the existing departments to cut taxes and skimp on public safety considerations.

"If they can show me on paper that we're going to have four men on an apparatus and two rigs in each house, I'd be more inclined to accept it," Michelin said, "but, so far, they've kept us and the public in the dark as to how (the new department) is going to run."

Legal efforts by Union City's fire rank-and-file and fire superiors unions to get the issue placed on a public referendum have thus far been stymied.

Fire unions are not the only opponents of the plan.

Guttenberg Mayor Peter LaVilla says his town can't afford to pay for the new system. LaVilla vetoed a town ordinance that will give the new department jurisdiction over its firehouses and equipment, but a Town Council majority voted to override it.

Thomas Canzanella, president of the Professional Firefighters Association of New Jersey, says regionalization is nothing short of a smoke screen for the "wholesale gutting" of municipal fire departments in North Hudson that he says has already happened in the last five years.

Canzanella cited the recent injury of a North Bergen firefighter while performing a rescue in Union City "that required several more firefighters to safely perform."

But Weehawken Public Safety Director Jeff Welz, who is heading an NHRFR transition team, countered that the merged departments will be positioned to send "almost double the number of firefighters you're seeing now" to a first alarm — without having to wait a critical "2 to 3 minutes" before calling in backup.

Ultimately, NHRFR plans to thin its ranks through attrition by offering an early retirement option to firefighters with seniority — if it gets legislative approval. An estimated 60 of the current 350 North Hudson firefighters could qualify.

If all 60 decide to leave, union leaders say that could leave the new department with a gaping hole to fill. Turner concedes the attrition "may leave us too depleted" but says NHRFR is taking steps to be prepared by hiring new firefighters from an old state list of candidates who have already passed the test.

"We can't wait for the state to schedule a new test because sometimes it takes up to two years for a new list to come out," Turner said. "We have to be ready now."

AT A GLANCE

Here's a summary of what the newly created North Hudson Regional Fire and Rescue will comprise:

- Union City, West New York, North Bergen and Weehawken will be partners in the new venture.
- It will have 347 firefighters (including superior officers) and an estimated $25 million in total payroll costs.
- It will use 15 firehouses (including some double bays), 19 pieces of "first-line" fire engines and trucks and seven reserve units.

Source: North Hudson Regional Council of Mayors and 1997 consultant study by Carroll Buracker of Harrisonburg, Va.

Mayors OK merger

Continued from Page A1

that regionalization is a critical component to give tax relief.

"With this move," Sires said, "we will continue to give the most professional, safest fire protection in New Jersey."

But the transition won't happen overnight, cautioned Weehawken Mayor Richard F. Turner. "Full integration (of the four municipal fire departments) should happen within a year," he said.

As a first step, the mayors council voted to hire the Secaucus law firm of Chasan, Leyner, Tarrant & Lamparello as the new entity's general counsel at $75,000 a year, the Little Silver law firm of Murray, Murray & Corrigan as labor counsel, also at $75,000; Jersey City real estate appraiser Hugh A. McGuire Jr. at $60,000; and Secaucus public relations firm Strategic Media at $36,000.

Participating municipal governing bodies will be asked to introduce ordinances at special meetings on Wednesday agreeing to be partners in the new venture and to transfer all municipal firehouses and equipment to the new organization. Union City, West New York and Weehawken meet at 7 p.m. at their respective municipal buildings; North Bergen meets at noon.

Public hearings will be held in each community on Sept. 30.

Attorney Ralph Lamparello said he expects to know by Wednesday how much North Hudson Regional Fire and Rescue will have to pay the four municipalities for their firehouses and equipment.

Because the new entity lacks bonding power under the state Consolidated Service Act, how it's going to get that money isn't yet clear, Lamparello said. It may borrow the money through the Hudson County Improvement Authority or it may get it, up front, from the state, he said.

Lamparello said he also expects, by Wednesday, to have worked out a cost-sharing formula for the four municipalities. Variables like a community's property values, total land acreage and size of fire department may be factored into such a formula.

By Jan. 1 or soon after, North Hudson Regional Fire and Rescue will be hiring paid professionals to run the organization, setting a budget, implementing an organization table to determine the numbers and ranks of employees and negotiating uniform salary scales for those employees who are now covered by seven separate union contracts, Turner said.

The mayors sought to assure union representatives who attended yesterday's meeting that nothing would be done to dismantle the existing ranks of nearly 350 firefighters spread through the four communities.

"There will be no personnel reductions, no demotions of rank and no firehouse closings," insisted Union City Mayor Rudy Garcia.

"There is an ironclad commitment there will be no layoffs," Turner added.

Turner said the projected tax savings "will happen through attrition and greater efficiency in operations." Turner said any actual savings might not be seen for "a year or two."

North Bergen Firefighters Union President Dominick Marino — who with other union officials has consistently voiced complaints that several North Hudson fire departments ride understaffed — said his primary concern about regionalization is "how they divide up the towns (with firefighters and equipment and how many firefighters ride on the truck)."

Right now, Marino said, "several towns ride with a bare minimum of three on an apparatus."

Mayors OK fire merger

4 towns vote next; hearings Sept. 20

By Ronald Leir
Journal staff writer

UNION CITY — After talking about it for 20 years and after hiring two consultants to study it, the North Hudson Regional Council of Mayors yesterday voted to regionalize firefighting services in four communities.

The fire departments of Union City, West New York, North Bergen and Weehawken will be consolidated under one umbrella service called the North Hudson Regional Fire and Rescue, to be governed by a four-member board of mayoral appointees.

Secaucus, with an all-volunteer department, has chosen not to participate.

Guttenberg Mayor Peter LaVilla said he supports the concept, "but I don't know if it's feasible for us because we're torn between volunteers and paid firefighters." LaVilla said he would confer further with his Town Council on the issue.

West New York Mayor Albio Sires, chairman of the council, said: "Now we've come to an historic moment. . . . As we take the lead in New Jersey and probably in the country, anyone in New Jersey who is concerned with property taxes realizes

---

Guttenberg votes to join fire merger

Continued from Page A1

Then, to the shock of many, town attorney Richard Bowe came out with what was termed an amendment to the regionalization pact that included Guttenberg. Councilwoman Joanne Martin then introduced a resolution to join in the consolidated fire department. With only LaVilla and Councilwoman Maria Gesualdi opposed, the vote was taken, 4-2, to join North Bergen, Union City, Weehawken and West New York in a 25-year contract.

Guttenberg Volunteer Fire Chief Yves Saad said it "seemed to be a done deal."

He said he had been working with others on a plan for the department, but the council "left no margin for anything else."

Martin assured him that "paid members and volunteers are taken care of," Saad said, but "with politics the way they are up here, I can't be sure we'll be here."

LaVilla and Gesualdi voted against the resolution because they said they hadn't had a chance to read the contract. At least two other council members who voted for it admitted they hadn't read it either.

Former DPW Director Edward Huebsch was one of many residents who were furious at the council. "You didn't read the report," Huebsch said. "You didn't explain the plan to volunteers. You're a disgrace to the community. You're not part of this town."

LaVilla said he has no intention of signing the resolution when it comes to his desk.

"I want those four councilpersons to resign. They're negligent in their duties by virtue of the fact that they voted on a 25-year contract without reading the contract," LaVilla said.

"I'm still in shock, in limbo," said full-time Fire Chief John A. Knoetig. "We haven't seen the contract. We don't know what's going on."

LaVilla said he still wants the new regionalized department to explain why it would cost Guttenberg $1.5 million a year to participate. He said Guttenberg now spends between $500,000 and $600,000 a year on firefighting services, including six paid firefighters.

A major step in the consolidation of the departments was communications. In 1982, North Hudson created a joint fire alarm dispatching system covering the departments that are now one. In 1995, these separate departments agreed to a mutual aid pact that allowed them to respond into each municipality automatically with revised multiple alarm running assignments. This was another step closer to total consolidation.

In 1997, a consultant firm from Virginia studied the five departments and completed their report. Some recommendations were accepted, but others were rejected.

A transition group was formed with representatives from all municipalities, headed by retired West New York Fire Chief Robert Aiello. The committee, which included local politicians, agreed to pool their resources to create the third-largest fire agency in the state and the first in New Jersey to cover multiple towns.

A state "buy-out" bill, signed by Governor Christie Whitman, provided early retirement incentives for members that met the requirements. Approximately fifty members took advantage of the "buy-out" bill and retired which downsized the Department from 360 to 310 positions.

The North Hudson Regional Fire and Rescue is the culmination of the largest merger of municipal services in state history. Its leaders Robert Jones, Chief of Operations (former Union City Fire Chief); Anthony Presutti, Chief of Administration (former West New York Fire Chief); Michael DeOrio, Director of Operations (former North Bergen Fire Director); and Jeff Welz, Director of Administration (Weehawken Public Safety Director) were sworn in on January 4, 1999.

A week later, on January 11, 1999, North Hudson Regional Fire and Rescue held its inauguration ceremony at North Bergen Fire Headquarters located on Tonnelle Avenue, which would become Regional's Fire Headquarters until January 4, 2005, when Fire Headquarters was relocated to a new building on Port Imperial Boulevard in West New York. This would also become the quarters of a newly formed company, Squad 7 which was established to protect the ever growing waterfront region of North Hudson. Squad 7 was assigned to the Decon Task Force and RIC Team duties.

The responsibility for apparatus maintenance and other transition duties was given to North Bergen Apparatus Chief Peter Guinchini and the North Bergen Repairs and Transportation Division. This group of talented men, equipped with a new shop building and appropriate resources, was one of the most obvious decisions made by the new department. The Repairs and Transportation Division is well known for its work, and many fire departments, local and out-of-state, seek their advice.

The new fire department took over more than 50 vehicles, including firefighting apparatus manufactured by such companies as Mack, Ward 79, Seagrave, Pierce, Grumman, E-One, and Maxim. The NHRF&R and the Township of North Bergen have an "inter-local agreement," whereby the fire department pays the township a fee for use of its facilities, fuel, and other resources. Besides vehicle maintenance, the shops is also responsible for SCBA, generators, fans, pumps, extinguishers, radios, and hose and ladder repair.

All front-line and reserve firefighting apparatus were re-lettered with NHRF&R markings before the new fire department was officially established. Local engine and truck company numbers were eliminated and fire units operated with their North Hudson County radio designation until permanent company numbers were assigned. These radio numbers were placed inside the Maltese crosses on apparatus to make it easy for firefighters and officers from various jurisdictions to identify. During this time, all fire companies remained open and the duty chief in each municipality still covered his entire town's geographical boundaries on all alarms.

In the beginning, all firefighters continued to use their assigned apparatus from their municipality. The shops inherited the problems of vehicles from all five departments and, at some

Highrise apartment buildings located at the top of the Palisades Mountains in West New York, with Fire Headquarters below on Port Imperial Boulevard.

The Hills in North Bergen, New Jersey.

The Palisades in Weehawken, New Jersey.

point, the facility was jammed packed with apparatus. Some repairs were quick and others were timely. Fire apparatus mechanics from Union City and Weehawken were re-assigned to the North Bergen facility.

On January 13, 1999, at 212 Dodd Street in Weehawken, North Hudson Regional responded to a 2nd Alarm fire. This was marked as Regional's first official fire, which was under the command of former Weehawken Deputy Chief Raymond Ficken. The next day, on January 14, 1999, at 200 Paterson Plank Road in Union City, the Department responded to a 3rd Alarm under the command of former Union City Deputy Chief Robert Cabral.

On January 21, 1999, North Bergen's former Mask Service Unit (MSU) was reassigned from the Repair and Transportation Division on Tonnelle Avenue in North Bergen to Engine Company 8's quarters located on 49th Street and Broadway, in West New York. The MSU was equipped with a six-bottle cascade, which was designed by the North Bergen Repair and Transportation Division. Since the merger, the MSU has been upgraded to carry 12 complete air packs and 72 spare bottles.

Four days later, on January 25, 1999, Division 1 was established, with quarters located at 29th Street and Central Avenue. This was done in an effort to establish a better command structure. Due to a surplus of Deputy Chiefs on some platoons, this unit was initially referred to as Battalion 4 until the new Department numbering system took effect.

On May 12, 1999, North Hudson was broken up into three battalions, under the supervision of a duty Deputy Chief. At this time, Battalion 4 was renamed Division 1, the on duty Deputy Chief. For Incident Command purposes, on May 20, 1999, Division was renamed Deputy 1. Running assignments were changed and the closest fire companies would answer alarms, regardless of municipal boundaries. Fire companies received new numbers, with front-line engines numbered 1 through 14, and front-line truck companies numbered 1 through 5. Reserve apparatus continue in number sequence.

Also during this phase, two companies in "double houses," were disbanded. Former Weehawken Engine 3, located at 46th Street and Park Avenue and former Union City Truck 3 located at 43rd and Bergenline were closed. The manpower from both units were transferred to other companies throughout North Hudson.

Fire apparatus remained with members of the former fire departments that were familiar with their operation. Former West New York Engine 6's 1983 Mack MC/Grumman was in such bad shape that it was taken off the roster and replaced with a 1988 Spartan/Grumman/Tele-Squrt, which was a Reserve Engine 5 in North Bergen. Now, there is a Tele-Squrt apparatus in each battalion. The squirts are assigned to Engine's 4, 6, and 11.

Former Union City's 1973/90 Seagrave 1500 gpm pumper was transformed by the shops into a Brush Fire Unit. Besides the 500 gallon water tank, a portable 525 gallon water tank was mounted in the rig's former hose bed. The pumper is equipped with two booster hose reels and pre-connected trash lines.

The town of Guttenberg formerly operated with three volunteer companies, two engines and a truck. Six-full time members were assigned to Engine 1. These six firefighters were absorbed into the new department and Engine 1 was a full-time unit, known as Engine 12. Local officials agreed to maintain a volunteer engine and truck that answer alarms within the confines of this town of 10,000 residents.

The volunteers use a 1984 Mack MC pumper and a 1980 Seagrave 100 foot rearmount. The pumper was the last fully assembled Mack pumper, before Mack terminated its fire apparatus line. Guttenberg Truck Company 1's 1977 American LaFrance mid-mount was taken out-of-service before the merger due to a damaged aerial ladder. The Regional purchased the 1980 Seagrave, which was used by the volunteers. This rig saw original duty in Glenolden, Pennsylvania.

On July 1, 1999, Engine Company 14, a 1986 Spartan Grumman, (former West New York Engine 5) was disbanded and its members re-assigned. The firehouse was closed due to asbestos. The 1986 Spartan Grumman was reassigned to North Hudson Reserve Engine 14.

In August of 1999, Regional put its first Marine unit into service. Marine 1 was birthed at Port Imperial Boulevard and was originally manned by the crews of Squad 1. In August of 2002, when Engine 3 was moved from Jane Street in Weehawken to 19th Street and Willow Avenue, Engine 3 became the new home of Marine 1. In 2007, Marine 1, was renamed the Vincent Neglia, in honor of our fallen brother.

The position of the Safety Officer was created on May 18, 2000. It was housed at 16th Street and New York Avenue. The Mask Services Unit (MSU) was assigned to this new company. One captain on each shift was assigned to this new position. In March of 2001, the position of a Deputy Chief's Aide was established to assist the Deputy with all his staffing, paperwork and command board at the fire scenes. In August of 2002, the Deputy Chief's Aide was re-assigned to the Safety Officer and his title was changed to Command Technician. This move was made when the Safety Officer was reassigned to the Jane Street Firehouse in Weehawken, and was unable to ride alone.

In November of 2000, with the Retirement of Chiefs Robert Jones and Anthony Presutti, North Hudson Regional promoted Deputy Chief Edward Flood, formerly of Weehawken, to the position of Chief of Department.

In January of 2001, Chief of Department Edward Flood and Battalion Chief Frank Montagne, Chief of Rescue Services, selected sixteen members of the Department to form a new Rescue Company. These members were transferred to Ladder 1 at 16th Street and New York Avenue where they spent a year and a half training in confined space, building collapse, hi angle rescue, and auto extrication.

In June of 2001, North Hudson Regional purchased a New Jersey Transit Bus 2748 (1980 Flexible) from Newark Ferry Street barn for $400, which the shops converted into a Rest and Recuperation Unit (RAC). The RAC bus was originally stationed at Engine 3's quarters on 19th Street and Willow Avenue. The RAC unit first saw action in North Hudson on July 26, 2001, when it responded to a 4th Alarm fire on 25th Street and Bergenline Avenue in Union City.

On February 18, 2002, Engine 8 was disbanded and Squad 1 was formed in its place. This was done in anticipation of the new Rescue Company, which would open in August. Engine 7 on 47th Street and Palisade Avenue, in Union City was closed to allocate manpower for Rescue 1. Rescue was located at 46th Street and Park Avenue, in Weehawken, with Ladder 3 until January 2005, when Engine 12 located on 68th and Madison, in Guttenberg closed.

At this same time, Ladder 2 was relocated from 19th Street and Willow Avenue to 29th Street and Central Avenue. They were assigned Reserve Ladder 7, a 1986 Seagrave Tiller, to replace their 1990 Seagrave rearmount quint, which was reassigned to Reserve Ladder 7, due to the tight streets in their district. Engine 3 was assigned a 1990 Seagrave Squrt, which had been previously assigned to Engine 4; and Engine 3's 1995 Seagrave was reassigned to Engine 4.

In the Spring of 2002, due to the construction and closure of Pershing Road, temporary Engine 15, was established on the waterfront using New York Waterway's old mechanical garage and an office trailer. This company was manned from 06:30 until 20:00 by overtime personnel due to the excess traffic conditions caused

Weehawken Water Tower, Weehawken, New Jersey.

New York Waterway Ferry Terminal

New York skyline from New York Waterway Ferry Terminal.

by the construction. This company was disbanded on May 5, 2003, when Pershing Road reopened.

In October of 2002, the Department purchased a 2002 Pierce Dash 100' Tractor Drawn Aerial (TDA), which was assigned to Ladder 4, located at 60th Street and Tyler Place in West New York.

Chief of Department Edward Flood retired in April of 2003, and Deputy Chief Brion McEldowney, of West New York was sworn in as the fourth Chief of Department for North Hudson Regional.

In May 2003, the Guttenberg Volunteer Fire Department, which had still been active at this time, was disbanded, and the two apparatus which they possessed, Engine 502, a 1984 Mack, and a Ladder 523, a 1980 Seagrave, were taken over by North Hudson Regional and designated Reserve Engine 16 and Reserve Ladder 8.

On September 19, 2003, North Hudson Regional Fire and Rescue received a Fire Safety Trailer, which was a donated by the New Jersey Deputy Chiefs Association. The Fire Safety Trailer is used in conjunction with the Department's and each of the individual towns Fire Prevention Programs. Squad 6, Engine 1, and Engine 11 maintain the Fire Safety Trailer.

In February of 2004, Engine 10 was renamed Squad 10, and was added to the Rescue Task Force and RIC (Rapid Intervention Crew) Team duties. A month later, Engine 2 was renamed Squad 2 and was assigned to the Decon Task Force and RIC Team duties.

In July of 2005, the Department received two 2005 Pierce Dash 100' TDA, which were assigned to Ladder 2, located at 29th Street and Central Avenue in Union City and Ladder 5, located at 83rd Street and Kennedy Boulevard in North Bergen. Ladder 2's 1986 Seagrave was reassigned to Reserve Ladder 7 and Ladder 5's 1985 Maxim was disposed of.

At that same time, the Department also received two 2005 Pierce Enforcers, which were assigned to Squad 1, located at 49th Street and Broadway and Engine 5, located at 43rd Street and Bergenline Avenue. Due to weight restrictions in the firehouse where Engine 5 was located, the 2005 Pierce Enforcer was reassigned to Squad 2 at 16th Street and New York Avenue. Squad 1's 1993 Emergency One was reassigned to Squad 7, located on Port Imperial Boulevard in West New York, and Squad 7's 1994 Emergency One was reassigned to Reserve Engine 18. Squad 2's 1988 Mack CF was reassigned to Reserve Engine 17.

In May 2006, North Hudson Regional received a 1986 Spartan/PL Custom which was designated as Rescue 2. This was given to North Hudson through a grant from the State of New Jersey to form an Urban Area Security Initiative (UASI). This grant was

Hudson-Bergen Light Rail Station 49th Street and Bergenline Avenue, Union City, New Jersey.

Hudson-Bergen Light Rail Tunnel runs from Port Imperial in Weehawken, New Jersey, to 51st Street and Tonnelle Avenue in North Bergen, New Jersey.

formed through the United States Department of Homeland Security to increase the state's capabilities to combat any other terrorist actions or major catastrophes. North Hudson was chosen as one of the nine UASI response teams, which were trained together by New Jersey Task Force One Urban Search and Rescue Team.

Shortly after 05:00 on September 9, 2006, North Hudson Regional responded to a 5th Alarm fire at 1813 Bergenline Avenue. This will always be remembered in North Hudson as the day they lost one of their own, Firefighter Vincent Neglia. In August of 2007, the Department dedicated their new Marine unit in honor of Vinny. On September 9, 2007, to mark the first anniversary of his passing, the Department held a dedication ceremony at Engine

North Hudson Regional Fire & Rescue 1999-2009 53

13, located on 75th Street and Hudson Avenue, where a plaque was placed on the firehouse in memory of Vinny.

In an attempt to increase the Department's RIC team capacity, Engine 6 was renamed Squad 6 and was designated an additional RIC team. The designated RIC teams are Squad 2, Squad 6, Squad 7 and Squad 10. The Rescue Task Force consists of Rescue 1, Squad 1, Squad 10, Ladder 3 and Ladder 4. The Decon Task Force consists of Squad 2, Squad 7 and Ladder 1.

On January 2, 2008, Squad 10 and Rescue 2 were involved in a motor vehicle accident on 57th and Palisade Avenue, in West New York, while enroute to a reported Structure Fire on 58th Street and Hudson Avenue, in West New York. Seven members were taken to local area hospitals, and six were released that night. The seventh member, Captain Kirk Miick, sustained injuries, that forced him to take an early retirement. Rescue 2's 1986 Spartan/PL Custom was sent back to PL Custom to have a new cab mounted on it. When returned to the Department, in 2009, it was classified a 2008 model. Squad 10's 1993 Emergency One was damaged beyond repair, so it was disposed of. They were reassigned a 1984 Spartan Grumman, former Reserve Engine 14. In May 2008, the Department leased a 2001 American La France Rescue Pumper to be reassigned to Squad 10 for one year, and the 1984 Spartan Grumman was placed back in service as Reserve Engine 14.

In 2009, during the Department's 10th Anniversary year, the Department received two 2009 Impel pumpers and a 2009 Pierce Arrow XT 100' TDA. Squad 6, located at 43rd Street and Tonnelle Avenue, received an Impel pumper with a 61 ft squrt and Engine 5, located at 43rd Street and Bergenline Avenue received a standard Impel pumper. Squad 6's 1998 Grumman was reassigned to Squad 7, and Squad 7's 1993 Emergency 1 was reassigned to Squad 10, and Squad 10's leased American La France Rescue Pumper was then returned. The 2009 Pierce Arrow XT was assigned to Ladder 1, which had been using Reserve Ladder 6. Engine 5's 1988, is still in service pending the company's move.

While this Department has already achieved so much, there is still much more to achieve. When this Department was formed 10 years ago, we were five individual departments with five distinct personalities, but now have grown into one brotherhood with a common goal – to keep the residents of North Hudson safe. ("North Hudson Regional Fire & Rescue 1999-2009" history submitted by Battalion Chief Robert Duane, Captain William Demontreux, Captain Robert P. Morrison III, Honorary Battalion Chief Ron Jeffers and Kimberley Kingsbury.)

Improvements Through Regionalizing

In light of September 11, 2001, and the North East Blackout of August 14, 2003, US Airway Flight 1549 on January 15, 2009, we see the importance of North Hudson Regional Fire and Rescue (NHRFR) in large scale emergencies in the metropolitan area. With improvements in specialized task forces, new equipment and training, the Regional will try to make the demands of an ever changing world.

Lincoln Tunnel, circa 1955.

Lincoln Tunnel Helix taken from Lincoln Harbor, Weehawken.

North Hudson Regional Fire & Rescue 1999-2009

Amtrak Emergency Action

In 1999, North Hudson Regional Fire and Rescue became part of the Amtrak Emergency Action plan concerning Incidents at New York City Penn Station and the North River Tunnels.

A joint response by North Hudson Regional Fire and Rescue and New York Fire Department (FDNY) was formed and initiated in the event of an emergency. New York City Penn Station and the North River Tunnels provide a link up and down the North East Corridor transporting thousands of passengers on hundreds of Amtrak and New Jersey Transit trains daily.

The safety of these passengers is of utmost concern to all agencies involved. Amtrak Chief Gary Hearn was very proactive and instrumental in providing North Hudson with two command post locations, Weehawken and North Bergen, equipped with Base Station Consoles and twelve (12) portable radios.

The Communications equipment provided by Amtrak has increased our safety when operating in the North River Tunnels. Chief Hearn has also assisted North Hudson, Deputy Chief Nicholas Gazzillo, Battalion Chief Michael Oriente and FDNY Chief Officers with the creation of a joint Standard Operating Procedure concerning incidents at these facilities.

Chief Hearn has provided us with the necessary knowledge and tools to mitigate any type of incident, and he has conducted yearly training providing updates for North Hudson Regional Fire and Rescue.

It is because of these accomplishments, actions and continued support by Chief Hearn that in 2009, the North Hudson Regional Fire and Rescue Valor Committee has awarded Chief Gary Hearn as a North Hudson Honorary Battalion Chief.

(*"Amtrak Emergency Action" history submitted by Battalion Chief Michael Oriente and Chief Gary Hearn.*)

Amtrak Chief, Gary Hearn, and 3rd Battalion Chief, Michael Oriente.

Checking out the command post.

North Hudson Regional Fire & Rescue 1999-2009

Notable Incidents Published in Fire Engineering Magazine

High-Rise Fire Eight Floors Down
by Deputy Chief Montagne

North Hudson (NJ) Regional Fire and Rescue received a call at 2355 hours in December 2006 for a smoke condition on the 10th floor of a 50-story high rise. One minute later, we upgraded our response to a working fire. "Routine fire," you would say, but the 10th floor is eight floors below street level. Should you take the elevators down or walk down eight flights of stairs? Normally, if a fire is on the eighth floor or lower, companies would walk up and stop one to two floors below the fire and begin operations.

The Galaxy Towers presented us with a difficult challenge. Standing on the cliffs of West New York/Guttenberg, New Jersey, the Galaxy complex overlooks the Hudson River from the George Washington to the Verrazano Bridge. Self-sufficient in design, the complex includes five buildings consisting of three 50-story towers, two 10-story annex buildings, parking decks, a shopping plaza, and a mini park. There are approximately 1,050 apartments. Parking garages serve all buildings and are below street level.

The unique octagon-shaped architecture enables more residents of the three towers to enjoy the majestic views of the Hudson River and Manhattan. Building 4, nestled between Tower 3 and Tower 2, provides residents with a full view of the Empire State Building. Building 5 wraps between Tower 2 and Tower 1, with views of the Verrazano Bridge. Below the three Galaxy Towers is the Galaxy Mall. Consisting of restaurants, a movie theater, a pharmacy, a bank, a grocery store, a beauty salon, a dry cleaner, a dental office, a travel agency, and a day care center, the Galaxy is self-sufficient.

The Galaxy Towers are unique in design but a nightmare for firefighters. The street-level lobbies for all three towers are on the 18th floor. The lobbies consist of a concierge desk, elevators, two enclosed stairways, and a two-story open atrium. This leaves 10 stories below street level. The confusing part of a fire below grade in this structure is determining what building you are in. If you have a fire below grade in Tower 1, you must descend to the lower floors from Tower 2 and gain access to Tower 1 through Building 5.

How can you determine where you are? During a nonemergency situation, you can distinguish it by the color of the carpets—the carpet colors are different for each group of buildings that are connected. Scissor stairs and an indoor pool are additional concerns. Fire protection features are fire alarms and standpipe systems (at the time of construction, sprinkler systems were not required in the buildings).

All the structures, other than the mall, start at the foot of the Palisades on the Hudson shoreline and rise up to the height of the Cliffs, with the towers continuing 30 stories above. Because of this singular construction and layout, each of the tower floors has only two short sides off the elevator vestibule (on average, there are just eight to 10 apartments per floor), thus avoiding the long institutional-like hallways in most large apartment buildings. Buildings 4 and 5 are below street level and connect all the towers; this is where the confusion and difficulty exist for firefighters. There are no individual elevators for Buildings 4 and 5; you must access them from the towers. During emergency situations, you must transverse several fire doors and long hallways to access Buildings 4 and 5.

The first-alarm working fire consisted of five engines, two ladders, Rescue 1, Battalion 3, and Division 1. Squad 10 was first to arrive and established command in the lobby of Tower 3. Battalion 3 arrived and assumed command. Companies arriving were instructed to descend to the eighth floor from Tower 2 and transverse through Building 4 to Tower 3. This was the safest approach.

Division 1 arrived at Tower 3 and did a face-to-face debriefing with Battalion 3. Battalion 3 was then assigned as operations officer. Companies prepared for an offense attack from the ninth floor and encountered moderate smoke conditions. They forced

58 **Notable Incidents Published in Fire Engineering Magazine**

Live-Produce Store Fire Poses Unique Problems
by Deputy Chief Anthony Avillo

There are some jobs you never forget. Some you remember by virtue of a great rescue or a great stop. Others are memorable because of the sheer magnitude of the fire or the size of the building-and sometimes the size of the loss. Having parking lots named after you also seems to immortalize certain fires. Sometimes, you remember the incident because the unusual circumstances surrounding it make it a "once-in-a-career" fire. This is one of those responses.

The Occupancy

The fire building was an old one-story taxpayer of ordinary construction and approximately 25 feet wide by 80 feet deep. It was occupied by Marzigliano's, a live produce store in West New York, New Jersey, that for decades had been a staple on Bergenline Avenue, a long thoroughfare lined with stores and mixed commercial-residential occupancies. Bergenline Avenue runs from the Jersey City line on the south end and stretches northward through the municipalities of Union City, West New York, Guttenberg, and North Bergen, terminating at the Hudson-Bergen County line. This area is protected by North Hudson Regional Fire & Rescue (NHRFR). (In 1999, the fire departments of the four above-mentioned municipalities and the township of Weehawken merged to form NHRFR. NHRFR, located directly across the Hudson River from Manhattan, protects three out of the five most densely populated cities in the country, with more than 60,000 people per square mile. There is no such thing as a fire without severe exposure concerns. Bergenline Avenue is at the heart of population and exposure central.)

Customers could go to Marzigliano's to buy a live animal and have it slaughtered and prepared to take home to cook, or they could purchase a live animal and take it home. You can imagine what we were greeted with as we arrived at this fire scene in the middle of the afternoon, when many shoppers were out. Goats, sheep, chickens, ducks, and rabbits were evacuating into the middle of Bergenline Avenue. It looked something like Noah's Ark meets Animal House.

Animals Evacuating

One of the things I will remember most about this fire is the amount of on-the-spot improvisation and adaptation that took place to meet the needs of the incident. First, there was the need to control the livestock that was rapidly evacuating the structure; this operation necessitated a redeployment of personnel who otherwise would have been assigned other duties.

The second alarm was struck immediately. Quick-thinking firefighters used several small portable dumpsters as well as some 55-gallon drums to create a makeshift pen near the building. They placed all the animals they could catch in the pen, where they waited until the Humane Society responded. Some animals wandered the avenue and had to be corralled. There were also reports of civilians carrying away some of the animals. I vaguely remember seeing a civilian carrying a goat down the block as I was getting out of the Division car.

Fire Conditions On Arrival

On arrival, heavy smoke was issuing from the roof area and drifting across Bergenline Avenue. Arrival conditions indicated a delayed alarm; the fire appeared to have taken hold of the cockloft in the rear. A moderate amount of smoke was venting from the open front doors. It was also churning at the floor level, which indicated the possibility of a cellar fire. I asked the owner how to

---

The Galaxy Towers in Guttenberg.

entry into the apartment, encountered high heat and smoke, and were forced back to the stairwell because of high winds, which blew through the apartment and drove very hot gases/smoke into the hallway. Exterior conditions included violently swirling black smoke and flames shooting 20 feet out from the windows.

Companies forced back to the stairwell maintained their position. Additional attack crews positioned themselves to attack with the wind from an adjacent parking garage. A standpipe hose valve (in a garage hose cabinet) was located 75 to 100 feet away from the fire apartment's hallway entrance door, allowing firefighters to attack the fire from that location. This worked favorably as companies were able to advance the lines to control and extinguish the fire. Primary search of the apartment was positive: A young woman perished in the fire. The victim was identified as 32-year-old Wendy Burlingame. She was one of the surviving daughters of Charles Burlingame, a decorated aviator and the pilot of American Airlines Flight 77, which crashed into the Pentagon on September 11, 2001.

Third and fourth alarms were called to facilitate the personnel-intensive operation. We implemented the incident management system, with Staging, Resources, Rehab, and Search and Evacuation Post areas for the 30 floors above the fire.

The intensity of the fire was revealed during overhaul: The hallways were black and the concrete was spalled. The attack stairwell had large sections of concrete that also spalled on the floor above.

During the operations, residents made numerous phone calls to the police department and the concierge's desk, creating an overwhelming situation at the command post. I instructed both parties to prioritize the calls and provide instructions for their safety. The Search and Evacuation Post established above the fire began the arduous task of ensuring all occupants above the fire were safe. We prioritized and addressed calls throughout the fire.

("High-Rise Fire Eight Floors Down" story submitted by Deputy Chief Frank Montagne, Fire Engineering - May 2008)

get to the cellar; he said there was no cellar. I found this strange because of the age of the building and my knowledge of the buildings in the area. Skeptical about his denial of the existence of a cellar and wondering what we might find beneath this unusual occupancy, I sent a company to see if they could determine if there was a cellar. The report was negative, so we were able to concentrate on the fire in the cockloft.

The smoke in the interior was heavy at the rear, but there was no fire. Animals were still running around in a panic in the smoke. Conditions were very interesting in there. Later, fire began to drop down at the rear, as the roof and ceiling began to fail; however, in the early stages, the fire was confined to the cockloft.

It appeared that the fire had gotten a good head start: The store's staff tried to fight the fire without success before calling NHRFR. The garden hose on the roof attested to this fact. Someone apparently had been using a flammable solvent to clean a feather evacuation system that mechanically plucks chickens. This system, constructed of metal ductwork, not unlike a common HVAC system, pierced the ceiling, extended into the cockloft, and terminated at an accumulation point on the roof. It was obviously packed with highly combustible feathers and other debris, as was the cockloft area. The fire originated at roof level, where the work was being performed, and spread downward into the cockloft through the system's ductwork. No fire protection system was in place to protect the system, the structure, or occupants.

Exposures

As always in this area, there were exposure concerns. The fire building was a single story. Access into the building was through the front door and a door in the alley on the D side. It was decided not to use this side door, even though it was closer to the fire area, because the heavy roof equipment involved in fire was in close proximity to this doorway. The concentrated load over the main attack access and egress point presented a hazard. It was easier and safer to attack from the front and use the reach of the streams. Additionally, the alley was only about 10 feet wide; any operation conducted in that alley would be directly in the collapse zone of the D wall of the fire building.

Exposure B was an attached two-story mixed-use building of ordinary construction. A jewelry store was on the first floor. The owner understandably had security concerns, especially as the afternoon and evening wore on. The major issue with this building, however, was that the second floor, which was residential, had several windows that faced onto the roof of the fire building. Since the fire was in the cockloft and was breaking through the roof on arrival, these windows were a main focus in regard to exposure protection.

Exposure D was separated from the fire building by a 10-foot alley. Although this two-story mixed commercial-residential structure was of ordinary construction, a wood-frame addition at the rear on the second floor was imminently threatened by the fire venting from the roof at the rear. Since the wind was blowing toward exposure D, the vinyl siding was already melting.

Exposure C was a 12-story fire-resistive high-rise. A 35-foot courtyard separated it from the rear of the fire building. Because of the building construction and the distance from the fire, the only protection needed for this building was to close all the windows on the fire side. The West New York Police Department handled this task. The courtyard provided a strategic advantage for Command in that it not only separated the fire building and the exposure by a good distance, but it also allowed apparatus access on the side.

Responses And Operations

The first-alarm response to the fire consisted of four engines, two ladders, Rescue 1, the safety officer, the Command Tech, and a battalion chief. I responded as the deputy and incident commander.

During the day, from 0800 until 2000 hours, as the deputy, I am not required to respond until a working fire is confirmed. It is

Firefighters used portable dumpsters and 55-gallon drums to create a makeshift pen.

Exposure B was an attached two-story mixed-use building of ordinary construction.

Exposure D was separated from the fire building by a 10-foot alley.

Notable Incidents Published in Fire Engineering Magazine

my option. Since this call "sounded like something," I decided to respond with the first-alarm companies. In NHRFR, confirmation of a working fire also brings a fifth engine as well as the rapid intervention crisis (RIC) team. The fifth engine helps to front-load the initial on-scene personnel profile as well as provide some operational flexibility in the initial scene assignments addressed by the standard operating procedures. Each additional alarm brings another two engines, a ladder, and a battalion chief. This fire went to a third alarm, not only because of the need to address exposure and tactical reserve issues but also to bring personnel to evacuate the animals from the building.

In addition to the animals that had been evacuating, walls were lined with cages filled with live chickens, ducks, and rabbits. We were hoping that these cages might be on wheels, but they were not. Not only were they not portable, but they were bolted in place so that the animals had to be taken out of the cages one by one. It took more than six hours to evacuate all of the animals and turn them over to the Associated Humane Society of Hudson County.

Chickens are easily agitated. Scared chickens are downright vicious. Full turnout gear and face and hand protection were required. During the fire suppression operations, firefighters removed the animals, loaded the livestock into dog-style kennels, and carried them out to the civilian handlers. I assigned one of my company officers as supervisor of the Animal Rescue Group; he had once worked in the store and had experience in this area. Firefighter experience knows no boundaries. Always use it to your advantage.

After the fire was extinguished, the Humane Society took over the job. We kept a skeleton crew of companies to assist in removing the animals and maintain a fire watch.

The first-alarm companies worked in the fire building, exposure B, the roof, and just outside the alley between the fire building and exposure D. These companies were reinforced and relieved by the second-alarm companies. Two lines were stretched into the fire building for attack through the front door. A line was stretched to the second floor of exposure B to address the concerns of the windows facing on the roof of the fire building, and a line was placed at the entrance to the alley to protect the exposed wood-frame surface at the rear of the exposure D.

The second-due engine (Engine 5) established a water supply for the first-due Squad 1, operating as the attack engine. Squad 2, the fifth-due engine, established a second water supply on the opposite side of Bergenline Avenue. The first-due Ladder 4 raised the aerial to the roof of the fire building for ventilation operations. Rescue 1 conducted the primary search of the fire building. Both the primary and the secondary searches for human life at this fire were negative. Ladder 2, second-due, entered and evacuated the B side exposure.

Ladder 4 reported that fire was venting from the roof in the C/D portion of the roof near some heavy roof equipment. This was the site where the fire originated. The concern was that the old roof would not support the equipment for too long. Ladder 4 opened some natural openings on the roof and was attempting to cut a hole to localize fire spread. The crew encountered a spongy roof as it moved closer to the fire area.

During this same time, the reports from the interior confirmed that the fire was in the cockloft. The lines had advanced about halfway to the rear; there was a heavy smoke condition but no fire. The crews were having difficulty accessing the cockloft. The 2 1/2-inch streams were not penetrating the ceiling, and the support personnel with pike poles were having a difficult time getting openings into the ceiling. In the smoke, they thought that maybe they were encountering tin ceilings or even double-tin ceilings, not unusual for this area or type of building. Because of this difficulty, they could punch only some small inspection holes into the overhead, which allowed limited stream penetration into the cockloft. It turned out that the ceilings were made of Formica® over plywood. We had never encountered such a ceiling and could not see it in the smoke. The owner advised that this covering was used because of the animal blood and fluids present over much of

Firefighters loading livestock into dog-style kennels before giving them to the civilian handlers.

A line was placed at the entrance to the alley to protect the exposed wood-frame surface at the rear of the exposure D.

the area. The Formica®-covered ceilings and walls made cleanup easier, as did the concrete floors that were pitched toward a drain.

The crews overcame the ceiling-penetration problem by using chain saws to get the ceiling opened so that streams could be operated from a distance to keep the fire in the cockloft in the rear and prevent it from advancing. This operation took time. An A-frame ladder was brought in to accommodate the cutting of the Formica® and plywood.

These interior reports were coming to the command post at about the same time as the spongy roof reports. Based on the fact that the roof support and structure were being compromised by the fire and the presence of the dead loads in that area, I ordered that the evacuation tones be sounded and that the fire building and the roof be evacuated. I felt the risk of continuing the interior or roof operation was not worth the benefit of saving the old building.

The companies working in the interior evacuated, as did Ladder 4 from the roof. A roll call was taken; all personnel were accounted for. The companies previously operating in the interior and the Interior Division commander notified me at this time that there was a brick wall about halfway back in the interior separating the front service area from the rear slaughter area (for lack of a better term). They felt that they could operate in an interior defensive fashion on the safe side of this wall to keep the fire to the rear. Before evacuation, they had put a few inspection holes in the ceiling on the service side of the wall and found no fire traveling in the cockloft there. Their plan was to open the ceiling and expose the whole brick wall on the safe side and fight the fire from

Notable Incidents Published in Fire Engineering Magazine 61

there. After consulting with the battalion chief assigned as Interior Division commander, I decided to let them attempt this operation, provided they kept a keen eye on the fire's movement. I assigned the safety officer to keep an eye on this area as well, so we would keep it as safe as possible. We decided that since the fire was eating up the roof decking at the rear, vertically venting the roof, manual vertical ventilation would not be needed. This enabled me to keep personnel from operating on the roof in an unsafe area.

We placed additional lines on the roof of exposure B to hit fire and to assist in protecting the rear D exposure. This line had a better angle than the line operating in the alley; but, to be safe, I kept both lines operating. I also had a line positioned on the roof of exposure D in case the fire broke through the roof and further threatened the exposure. An interior protective line was also stretched into the wood-frame addition of the exposure. Since this was an add-on, the only access into this area was from a metal stairwell on the C side.

In addressing the C side of the structure, there were no windows or doors for stream penetration or ventilation opportunities. It was decided to place Engine 11, a telescoping waterway, in the courtyard to be used in a defensive fashion to address fire venting through the roof. This stream was readied but was not used initially because we did not want to drive fire back into the building. We waited for more of the roof to burn away. A third water supply was established to supply this master stream. A Division C commander was assigned to the rear. These were third-alarm companies.

We now had the fire surrounded, and it was matter of coordinating the operations of the companies behind the brick wall on the interior with the master streams at the rear and the streams from the roof. Ladder 4 officer, assigned as the B Roof Division commander, coordinated stream operations with the other assigned division commanders. There was some minor extension into the service area through some unprotected breaches in the brick wall; however, since it was open, companies were in position to quickly contain this spread. They used pike poles, chain saws to open the ceiling, and a well-coordinated and disciplined handline operation.

While these exterior/interior defensive stream operations were underway, the animal evacuation operation continued. Since the lines on the interior were behind the cages lining the walls, they protected the companies conducting the animal-removal operation.

One of the problems we encountered with the stream operations was that the runoff was accumulating in the sloped drainage areas that happened to

A metal stairwell on the C side which was the only access into the wood-frame addition of the exposure.

The third-alarm companies and Division C commander assigned to the rear of the structure.

Notable Incidents Published in Fire Engineering Magazine

The runoff from the stream operations accumulated in the sloped drainage areas in proximity of the animal cages.

Ladder 4 was used to see what was going on at roof level.

be in proximity to the animal cages. As a result, the water became contaminated with feces, feathers, and other nastiness. To address this concern, a Decon Group was established. A small-diameter line was set up on the exterior on the A side; anyone working in the interior was ordered to be decontaminated after exiting the structure. All personnel who operated at this fire were encouraged to fill out NHRFR hazardous exposure reports so that the incident and the offending material could be properly documented. Further, the Department of Health was requested to respond early in the incident to evaluate the hazards. In addition, we put into service three sump pumps to remove the water building up in the area.

As expected, a good portion of the roof collapsed at the rear. Since the building was old, the roof had been built up for many years with tar and roofing material. As a result, fire was hiding under the collapsed roof decking and was not burning away the roof as quickly as we would have liked. The interior defensive operation was successful: The fire did not pass the brick wall. However, it appeared from below that only a small portion of the roof had collapsed in the slaughter area because the plywood and Formica® ceiling was so strong that the roof collapse did not collapse the ceiling, except at the rear. Thus, the ceiling in most areas other than for the extreme rear of the building, was intact. The interior companies were considering the idea that it would be safe to move in to cut away the ceilings to finish extinguishment after the exterior streams had been shut down. Fortunately, they communicated these plans to the exterior companies. As it turned out, the view from the exposure roofs was quite different. The interior companies were informed that they should not pass the brick wall and attempt to expose and extinguish fire burning above what they thought was an intact ceiling. We had to move a few well-intentioned, but misinformed, companies out of the area in the early stages of the overhaul phase. For the most part, however, the Interior Division companies stayed behind the brick wall. Good communication and disciplined operations always bring about better coordination on the fireground.

I was also able to get a better feel for the operation by virtue of a Command transfer. The protocol for NHRFR is that when a third alarm "doubtful" is issued during the progress report, as was the case here, the chief of the department responds and takes command of the incident. The deputy then is assigned as Operations Section chief. The advantage of this move, especially at this fire, is that you are no longer shackled to the command post. I was able to do a personal reconnaissance to get a better idea of the operation and to understand what was happening on the fireground.

I first climbed Ladder 4's aerial to see what was going on at the roof level. From there, I could see the extent of the failed roof and the dead loads in those areas. It was more extensive than what could be seen from the interior. I now understood the gravity of the radio transmissions going from the roof to the interior. I quickly looked at the interior and consulted with the Interior Division commander relative to my concerns. Things seemed to be under control there.

I then went to the rear and climbed the telescoping waterway to survey the amount of fire still confined under the fallen roof. To extinguish it, we would have to access it from the interior or from the exterior somehow; access from the interior was not possible because of the danger of a secondary collapse

Access from the C side also was not possible unless we breached a wall, which was not worth the effort at this stage of the fire. To bring in demolition crews to remove the rear wall to access and finish extinguishment was also not an option, as the Building Department declared the building sound except for the roof and a candidate for rebuilding. There would be no tearing out of the rear wall. Another option quickly discussed and just as quickly dismissed was to let the fire burn through the rest of the roof. It was decided that if we waited for that to happen, we would be there forever.

We instead opted to bring the ladder of the telescoping waterway to roof level and to work from the safety of the ladder to slice inspection holes in the portions of the roof still attached to the rear wall. The bulk of the hidden fire was concentrated under this area. We then placed a distributor in the hole and let it operate, alternating between holes for the remainder of the fire and the fire watch. Along with the line on the roof of exposure B that was hitting visible hot spots, it did the job. By the next morning, there were no remaining hot spots.

Another issue that competed for the attention of Command was the circus-like atmosphere in the area. This was a major newsworthy as well as a civilian-heavy event. You don't see farm animals running down a busy intersection in the middle of an urban area every day. As a result, the press was everywhere: in the streets, in helicopters, and generally in the way with their cameras. We quickly used the police to establish and maintain a civilian

Notable Incidents Published in Fire Engineering Magazine

safety perimeter. We also set up a press staging area, where reporters could take their pictures and be briefed and updated by NHRFR officials. One of our directors operated as press liaison and coordinated interviews with the incident commander and other players in this incident.

In the end, the building was saved, the exposures were undamaged, and scores of livestock were removed from harm and transported to shelters.

(*"Live-Produce Store Fire Poses Unique Problems" story submitted by Deputy Chief Anthony Avillo, Fire Engineering – January 2007*)

U.S. Airways Flight 1549 New Jersey Rescue Operations
by 2nd Battalion Chief Michael Cranwell

On January 15, 2009, at 1530 hours, US Airways Flight 1549, an Airbus A320, made an emergency landing in the middle of the Hudson River, abeam of the NY Waterways commuter ferry terminal in Weehawken, New Jersey. Passengers evacuated the aircraft, taking refuge on the wings and in rafts.

The North Hudson Regional Fire Communications Center received multiple calls reporting the ditching. At 1534 hours, a North Hudson (NJ) Regional Fire & Rescue (NHRFR) first-alarm assignment (four engines, two ladders, one heavy rescue, one battalion chief, one deputy chief, and one safety officer) was dispatched to 1 Pershing Road (Arthur's Landing) in Weehawken on the Hudson River waterfront, about a quarter-mile south of the ferry terminal.

En route, Deputy Chief David Curtis directed the communications center to notify the Fire Department of New York and ordered deployment of NHRFR's 32-foot fire boat, Marine 1, moored a quarter-mile south of the incident. I responded as the first-due battalion chief, arriving on the scene just as Curtis was getting out of his car. All we knew in those first few moments was that a large aircraft was down in the water and that a boat was approaching the dock with victims. We needed to know much more and to get the right resources to this incident.

The Pershing Road Command was set up in the valet parking area of the Arthur's Landing Restaurant.
Photo right: *(l. to r.) Deputy Chief David Curtis, Chief Brion McEldowney, and 2nd Battalion Chief Michael Cranwell.*

Four minutes earlier, I had been responding to a routine alarm malfunction at a local grammar school when the radio alarm was transmitted for an aircraft down in the Hudson River. Within 60 seconds, I was headed toward one of the most extraordinary runs in my 35 years on the job. Approaching the waterfront, I saw a dozen people on the sidewalk along the chest-high wall, pointing toward the river. But I couldn't see what held their attention, just the disheartening expressions of grief on their faces.

As a licensed private pilot, I was familiar with the airspace above the Hudson River, a high-density air corridor. Flights arriving and departing from the area's three major airports, Newark Liberty International, John F. Kennedy International, and LaGuardia, within a radius of 20 miles make this one of the most congested

Notable Incidents Published in Fire Engineering Magazine

Three FDNY fireboats, the NHRFR fireboat, and three civilian ferries removing survivors from the aircraft.

airspaces in the nation. I also knew that the Hudson River is a major air corridor for general aviation, since I have flown through this corridor many times myself. Driving down to the river, I thought the "plane down" was likely to be a light aircraft. The first engine company's radio report, indicating a large passenger jet was involved, was utterly discouraging. I anticipated a catastrophic outcome.

Pershing Road Command

At 1537 hours, Squad 7 established command and transmitted its initial on-scene report stating that they observed a "large jet in the middle of the river." The squad was joined at the dock by seven police officers from the Weehawken Police Department (WPD) and the Port Authority of New York & New Jersey Police Department (PAPD). At 1538 hours, Curtis and I arrived on scene, along with Squad 1, Engine 5, and the safety officer.

No one knew what had disabled the aircraft, but it was obvious that many people had evacuated the aircraft and needed to be rescued. According to initial reports, 146 passengers were aboard the flight; it was later confirmed as 155.

We set up the Pershing Road Command in the valet parking area of the Arthur's Landing Restaurant. Officers from NHRFR, the Weehawken Office of Emergency Management (OEM), the WPD, and the PAPD conferred, initiating the unified command process. That conference established the following goals:

- Restrict scene access to emergency responders.
- Set passenger rescue as the utmost priority; responders would coordinate with New York City emergency services in the rescue effort.
- Obtain emergency medical service (EMS) resources for a mass-casualty incident.
- Provide immediate medical attention and a private, secure sheltered area for rescued passengers.
- Account for the survivors, and initiate victim tracking.
- Acquire and manage the flow of more detailed information.
- Cooperate with investigating agencies such as the National Transportation Safety Board.

Command immediately designated the NY Waterways ferry terminal the Ferry Division, which would be the primary receiving point to accept and triage the more than 100 victims who were expected to be sent to New Jersey; Command also ordered EMS and police personnel to the ferry terminal to receive the victims. NY Waterways was directed to send its New Jersey-bound ferries to the terminal.

Command requested NHRFR to strike a second alarm, which brought NHRFR Battalion 3, Ladder 4, and Rescue 1 to the ferry terminal. Battalion 3 Chief William Valentine was named the Ferry Division supervisor, responsible for coordinating the emergency response at the ferry terminal, working with EMS in attending and tracking rescued passengers at the terminal, and interacting with law enforcement.

Anticipating a large influx of victims, Command assigned NHRFR Battalion Chief David Barth to assist Valentine. Hudson County EMS Coordinator Mickey McCabe, assigned as EMS Branch director, supervised EMS operations at the ferry terminal.

The restaurant at 1 Pershing Road (Arthur's Landing), a quarter-mile south of the terminal, was designated as the sheltered triage center for the first victims who were then disembarking there. Battalion Chief Mike Giacumbo was assigned as the victim tracking officer at the restaurant.

The Rescue

Because of the quick decision making and the exceptional airmanship that Flight 1549's Captain Chesley B. Sullenberger demonstrated, passengers were able to self-evacuate the aircraft. They took refuge on the wings of the plane and in rafts deployed from the plane. The air temperature was 20°F; the water temperature, 36°F.

Even before police and fire rescue units arrived, the captains of several NY Waterways ferries, recognizing the emergency, redirected their courses toward the plane to render aid. These quick-thinking ferry captains and their crews performed superbly and were commended for their heroic efforts in the rescue.

Notable Incidents Published in Fire Engineering Magazine

Emergency responders from New York and New Jersey converged on the sinking aircraft and accomplished an expedited rescue operation.

At 1540 hours, the NHRFR Squad 1, Squad 7, and Engine 5 crews, along with WPD and the PAPD police officers, boarded the NY Waterways ferry Henry Hudson, moored at Arthur's Landing. Within two minutes, the vessel was heading toward stranded passengers in a raft at the tail of the aircraft. They were the first of New Jersey's emergency services to reach the aircraft. Squad 1's officer transmitted a radio report informing Pershing Road Command that three FDNY fireboats, the NHRFR fireboat, and three civilian ferries were removing survivors from the aircraft.

The Henry Hudson was soon joined by more NY Waterways ferries, multiple vessels from FDNY and the New York Police Department (NYPD), a Circle Line sightseeing boat, NHRFR Marine 1, two U.S. Coast Guard boats, and later New Jersey State Police (NJSP) boats. Directed and coordinated by the U.S. Coast Guard (USCG), the rescue operation was completed swiftly; within 40 minutes, the airliner's rescued passengers and crew were on shore. Although the outgoing tide was moving the aircraft south on the river at 10 knots, this did not hinder the operation since the rescue boats were also moving with the tide.

By 1544 hours, two USCG rigid-hull inflatable boats arrived at Arthur's Landing. At 1555 hours, NHRFR Squad 1 reported to Pershing Road Command that divers had entered the aircraft's cabin and verified that it had been completely evacuated. Emergency service boats continued to search the river for additional victims.

At 1557 hours, NHRFR Rescue 1 personnel boarded another NY Waterways ferry along with advanced life support (ALS) EMS units, departing from the terminal to participate in the rescue effort. At 1600 hours, the Rescue 1 officer relayed reports from FDNY water rescue units that all passengers had been accounted for.

EMS Response

Jeff Welz, director of Weehawken Public Safety, codirector of NHRFR, and the Weehawken municipal emergency management coordinator, arrived on the scene just as Squad 7 was transmitting its initial report. With a 35-year background in public safety and a close affiliation with three key agencies already on the scene, Welz was uniquely qualified to coordinate the response of fire, police, and EMS and liaison with the state and county offices of emergency management. With the rescue of so many survivors then underway, Welz activated the Hudson County EMS Mutual Aid Plan, immediately bringing in 25 EMS units from around the county to cope effectively with this mass-casualty incident. These units responded to an EMS staging area at the scene.

Anticipating the need for even more EMS participation, the New Jersey EMS Task Force was also mobilized but only partially deployed. Additional EMS units, primarily from Bergen and Essex counties, were also mobilized and directed to stage at Giants Stadium in East Rutherford, six miles from Weehawken, but were not deployed.

It was quickly decided that the optimal location for disembarking large numbers of rescued survivors would be the NY Waterways ferry terminal, located a quarter-mile north of the command post. This spacious facility is on Port Imperial Boulevard, a two-lane north/south roadway that parallels the Hudson River. A two-lane access road from the boulevard accommodates normal commuter dropoffs and pickups.

This choice was ideal. The police could easily clear and secure the terminal, and multiple EMS vehicles could stage close by and then drive directly to the front of the terminal without tying up traffic on Port Imperial Boulevard. As the ferry boats arrived at the terminal, the victims could be taken immediately indoors to the warm triage area. The ferry terminal is also just two miles south of the Palisades Medical Center in North Bergen, which has a quick-response emergency department that includes a heliport.

The first of the two USCG rigid-hull inflatable boats arrived at the Arthur's Landing dock near the command post with 10 passengers, followed by a second one with nine more. Emergency responders on the dock escorted them into the nearby Arthur's Landing Restaurant. EMS units initially responded to this site, where they triaged and treated victims for nonlife-threatening injuries, mostly minor cuts, scrapes, and bruises. Subsequent arriving EMS units were directed to the NY Waterways Ferry Terminal, where large numbers of victims could be better accommodated and attended to. EMS provided triage, treatment, and tracking at both locations.

EMS provides triage and treatment for victims of the crash.

NY Waterways ferries subsequently brought 42 more passengers to the main ferry terminal. EMS immediately took three of these passengers to the hospital for treatment of possible hypothermia. While law enforcement provided security, EMS immediately evaluated the remaining 58 passengers at the ferry terminal and at the restaurant. Because of the air and water temperatures, these survivors were wet and cold. They were treated primarily for hypothermia, minor cuts, and bruises. The Red Cross provided blankets, and NHRFR provided disposable redress garments.

Incredibly, none of the 155 passengers and crew of Flight 1549 sustained life-threatening injuries. Sixty-one passengers were taken to the New Jersey side of the Hudson River. At 1715 hours, they were bused to the Weehawken Senior Citizen Nutrition Center, where they were reunited with loved ones.

Victim Tracking And Assistance

An accurate accounting of all those aboard Flight 1549 was vital to confirm that everyone had been rescued. This was complicated, since victims were taken to sites on both sides of the river. The victim-tracking data from New Jersey, essentially the arriving passengers' names and seat assignments, were quickly passed to Deputy Chief Curtis at the command post. This information was relayed to the NHRFR dispatchers in West New York, who communicated by landline with the FDNY Fire Operations Center, which had access to the US Airways passenger list.

Initially, there was some confusion regarding two toddlers who were onboard the flight, because they did not have their own seat assignments. Both toddlers were located at the Weehawken ferry terminal along with their mother, and this information was passed on to FDNY.

When the last victim had been transported from the ferry terminal, the Weehawken OEM, EMS, and PAPD conferred to definitively verify that all passengers and crew of Flight 1549 had in fact been accounted for. The PAPD had obtained the passenger list from US Airways at LaGuardia Airport, where the flight originated.

As the first group of dazed passengers stoically disembarked from the USCG boat and walked past me on the dock, I told them, "We're going to get you into a safe and warm place." We took the opportunity to connect personally with these passengers. The victim tracking officer, Giacumbo, had a much more personal connection with many of the passengers assembled inside Arthur's Landing Restaurant. He had to quickly get the survivors' names and seat assignments and pass the information on to Command.

Giacumbo did his job methodically and expeditiously and continued helping these people. One passenger had been traveling with his adult son. In the mayhem, they had been separated. The father did not know his son's fate and feared the worst. Giacumbo worked tenaciously to get solid confirmation that this man's son was safe and in good health on the New York side. The cross-checking and verifying process took 40 minutes; Giacumbo wanted to have accurate and reliable information from a credible source before he passed the word on to this worried father. During this agonizing 40-minute interval, this inconsolable passenger was emotional and pleading for any information. It was disheartening when Giacumbo repeatedly could only tell this gentleman, "We're working on it." When Giacumbo was satisfied he had located the man's son, the father was genuinely grateful; his relief and joy were shared by all involved.

North Hudson firefighters leave NY Waterways Ferry after assisting in the Hudson River.

Naturally, these passengers were anxious to talk with their loved ones. Since they exited the aircraft so quickly, many left their cell phones aboard the plane. NHRFR Firefighter Frank Martinez of Squad 1, who had assisted EMS with triage, offered the use of his personal cell phone to any passenger who needed it. Half a dozen passengers gratefully accepted, including one woman who wanted to call her mother in Australia. She later returned the phone with deep appreciation. Martinez was gratified that he could help.

These are but two examples of the compassion emergency responders displayed that afternoon, among many others.

Preplanning Drills

NHRFR anticipated the need to rescue a large number of people from a craft on the Hudson River. In early 2002, the department considered the problems a developing waterfront community and an expanding passenger ferry service in Weehawken presented. To address these concerns, NHRFR conducted two drills with NY Waterways, an initiative the ferry service's management supported enthusiastically. All concerned recognized that a mass-casualty incident on the Hudson River would present unique challenges.

On August 21, 2002, emergency responders conducted a full-scale drill, simulating a collision between a passenger ferry and another large vessel. This scenario called for a large number of injured civilians on the ferry and also incorporated the simultaneous challenge of fighting a fire onboard the vessel. NY Waterways, NHRFR, FDNY, NYPD, NJSP, and USCG all contributed assets to this drill. Subsequently, the USCG was designated the lead agency that would control and coordinate any emergency response on the Hudson River.

Operations Assessment

The first responders—fire, police, EMS, and OEM personnel—worked diligently to achieve common goals. This rapidly evolving incident quickly moved through three fundamental phases: rescue; triage-treatment-transport; and law enforcement-investigation. When these phases overlapped, life safety always took precedence. New York City responders addressed incident stabilization by securing the aircraft and environmental concerns regarding aircraft fuel.

No single entity had the capability to meet this challenge alone. This incident required the talent and resources of many agencies but in varying degrees, at varying intervals, and in the proper sequence. This reinforced the need and value of an effective command structure. Each emergency service involved had a significant role; as the incident evolved, each agency's level of involvement similarly evolved.

Civilian involvement was vital. NY Waterways civilian personnel played a key role in rapidly and successfully rescuing such a large number of people. Similarly, the civilian staff at Arthur's Landing Restaurant and in the Weehawken Ferry Terminal helped provide a secure and warm shelter for those rescued and was a most welcome contribution.

The biggest shortcoming was the lack of direct communication among the New Jersey and the New York command posts and the USCG. Communication between the New Jersey command post and the FDNY incident commander was too cumbersome. Messages were relayed through NHRFR fire dispatchers, through PAPD, and through NHRFR personnel aboard boats at mid-river who were communicating with FDNY, NYPD, and USCG boats at the aircraft. Although workable, this process was certainly not the most expedient.

Several variables worked in our favor. The incident occurred in daylight; the weather was cold but precipitation-free; and the river was relatively calm, lacking the normal chop and ice. Ferries were staffed and ready since they were preparing for the evening's weekday rush-hour commute.

This emergency landing and the ensuing rescue operation has been universally acclaimed as the most successful incident of its type. Everyone aboard Flight 1549 was quickly and efficiently rescued without any life-threatening injuries. NY Waterways personnel performed magnificently. EMS promptly treated and triaged all 61 victims taken to New Jersey. The New Jersey State EMS MCI plan was well executed in a timely manner. New York City agencies attended the remainder of the passengers on the New York side of the Hudson.

However, since rescued passengers were taken to various locations, victim tracking/accountability was difficult.

(*"U.S. Airways Flight 1549 New Jersey Rescue Operations"* story submitted by Battalion Chief Michael T. Cranwell, *Fire Engineering* – July 2009)

Night of Fire
December 1, 2001

December 1, 2001, was a night that many North Hudson firefighters will never forget.

The 2nd Platoon was on duty when a reported structure fire at 3114 Tonnelle Avenue in North Bergen was reported around 2130 hrs. Units on the scene reported heavy fire in a 3-story ordinary mixed occupancy structure with extension to two attached 3-story similar buildings. The fire would go to four alarms before being declared under control around 2330 hrs. Companies returned to the firehouse and readied their tools and equipment for the next run.

At approximately 0015 hrs., a reported structure fire came in for 1016 Summit Avenue in Union City. Engine 1 and Ladder 1 arrived at the same time. Ladder 1's officer transmitted a 2nd alarm on arrival for fire in a 3-story ordinary mixed occupancy with people trapped on the upper floors. Due to these conditions, Ladder 1 transmitted the 3rd alarm. Deputy Chief Eric Inauen transmitted the 4th alarm due to heavy fire in the fire building and two attached exposure buildings. After the roof man of Ladder 1 Company 1 vented the fire building and he reported seeing another fire about a block away.

At this time, Fire Control notified command that they were transmitting a full assignment for a fire at 10th & West Street's in Union City. A recall chief in Battalion 4 reported a fully involved 3-story wood-frame dwelling. He requested a 2nd alarm on arrival. This fire would also go to 4th alarm before being brought under control.

A company responding to the second 4th alarm was stopped at the 400 block of 13th street where a civilian reported another fire. The first arriving company confirmed a fire on the outside of a 2-story frame dwelling with an extension to the building. That company transmitted a 2nd alarm.

Due to the radio traffic on two channels being used, Deputy Chief Inauen, at the first fire, could not confirm that a chief responded to the third fire. He was relieved at the first fire by Chief of Department Edward Flood. Previously, D.C. Inauen had given his car to an off duty fire captain to pick up manpower. He could not find his car so he commandeered a taxi to take him to the third fire. This fire would also go to 4 alarms. The alarm makeup included Secaucus Engine 1, Harrison Truck 1 and F.D.N.Y. Engines 5 and 34, Tower Ladder 21 and the 7th Battalion Chief.

In addition to this mutual aid response, F.D.N.Y. Ladder 3 and Ridgefield Tower Ladder 1 were sent to and operated at the Summit Avenue fire. Later, F.D.N.Y. Engine 5, Battalion 7 and Division 3 also reported to Summit Avenue.

It should be noted that calling the F.D.N.Y. across the Hudson River is highly unusual. Under normal circumstances, mutual aid would be summoned from bordering Jersey City; however, that department was operating at a fatal multiple-alarm that struck before the Summit Avenue fire was transmitted.

Also during these incidents, the fire at the first 4th alarm on Tonnelle Avenue, North Bergen, flared up and required a first-alarm assignment to extinguish. This assignment included mutual aid rigs from Bayonne, Ridgefield and Fort Lee.

Night of Fire December 1, 2001 69

North Hudson Regional Fire & Rescue Badges

North Hudson Regional Fire & Rescue
Personnel

Chief & Staff

Brion W. McEldowney
Chief

David J. Barth
Battalion Chief Fire Prevention/
Community Relations

David Donnarumma
Battalion Chief Training

Michael J. Giacumbo
Battalion Chief Special Operations

Robert R. Reed
Captain Supplies & Maintenance

William J. Fischer
Firefighter Chief's Aide

72 **Chief & Staff**

Deputy Chiefs

Anthony L. Avillo
1st Platoon

Nicholas Gazzillo
2nd Platoon

Frank C. Montagne
3rd Platoon

David Curtis
4th Platoon

Battalion Chiefs

First Platoon

Frank A. Vasta
1st Battalion

Steven Quidor
2nd Battalion

Michael Falco
3rd Battalion

Second Platoon

Richard Laterra
1st Battalion

Daniel F. Giacumbo
2nd Battalion

Michael Oriente
3rd Battalion

Battalion Chiefs

Third Platoon

Charles R. Thomas
1st Battalion

Robert J. Duane
2nd Battalion

John G. Halpin, Jr.
3rd Battalion

Fourth Platoon

Marc Johnson
1st Battalion

Michael Cranwell
2nd Battalion

William C. Valentine
3rd Battalion

Safety Officers

Brian McGorty
1st Platoon

Dominic P. Sico
2nd Platoon

George J. Lang
3rd Platoon

Martin Sanzari
4th Platoon

Thomas W. Irving
Retired 10-01-2009
3rd Platoon

Command Technicians

Randy J. Cosentino
1st Platoon

Alan M. Cody
2nd Platoon

Joseph Candeloro
3rd Platoon

Perry Rivera
4th Platoon

76 **Safety Officers & Command Technicians**

Captains

Robert Agostini

Alan Ballester

Sergio Barreto

Brian Boele

Scott M. Broking

Leonard Calvo

Leonel Calvo

Peter A. Camaiore

Patrick Cardinali

Edward V. Connors

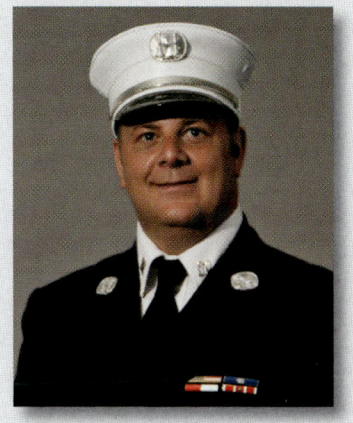

Anthony Cospito

Alan Dembroe

William Demontreux

Richard Desimone, Sr.

Mario Di Pietro Jr.
Retired 11-01-2009

Eduardo L. Diaz

Captains 77

Captains

James J. Donnelly  | Fred Fede  | David Flood  | Marc A. Franco

Keith R. Gonyou  | Stephen J. Hegarty  | Michael P. Hern  | Richard J. Hess

Marco Indri  | Joseph F. Isola  | Samuel L. Isola  | Anthony Jones

Paul Kirchoff  | Frank Kiszka Jr.  | Eugene La Mastro
Retired 11-01-2009 | William Laban

Captains

Captains

James W. Lemke

William J. Lemonie

Mark R. Lorenz

Dominic B. Lorenzo

Michael P. Martin

Mark E. Masterson

James McDonough

Scott Marione

Sean T. McLellan

Kirk Miick
Retired 01-31-2009

Sean W. Miick

Robert P. Morrison III

Gary R. Mureo
Retired 07-31-2009

Drew C. Newcomb

John O'Sullivan

Walter Paczkowski
Retired 05-01-2009

Captains

Herman Peters

Robert Pisani

Stephen P. Polcari

Kevin M. Riley
Retired 04-01-2009

William J. Ring

Rory Rivera

Jose Rodriguez

Dominic Rovito

Dennis J. Rudd

Jonathan Rush

Carlos Schlaffer

Timothy J. Steinel

James J. Stelman

Sean P. Sullivan

Richard Testa

Thomas Tormey, Jr.

Captains

Captains

Moises Valdes

Victor Vangelakos

Anthony Venezia

Eric Winters

John E. Woltmann
Retired 10-31-2009

William C. Woltmanm
Retired 08-31-2009

Squad 2 at 3rd alarm, 301 45th Street with Macy's 4th of July fireworks display over the Hudson River.

Captains 81

Firefighters

Rafael Albarran

Thomas Altomare

Michael Alvarado

Steven Alvarez

Alain Amaro

Darren M. Anacker

John Antommarchi

Joseph P. Arena

Manuel Arenal

Fernando Astralaga

Francis Baker, Jr.

Alexander Banoff

Richard Barreres, Jr.

David Barreres

Brian Barreto

Luis Bodega

Firefighters

Firefighters

Damon Bodziak

Desmond Boyle

Matthew Caliente

Joseph A. Caruso

Vincent Caruso

Anthony S. Casper

Kory Cocciadiferro

Michael Cocciadiferro
Retired 05-01-09

Timothy Colacci

Raymond W. Colavito

Jaime Concepcion

Kevin Corbo

James Corso

Brian M. Cosentino

Patrick Cospito

Kevin Cowan

Firefighters 83

Firefighters

Patrick Cowan	Philip Cranwell	Michael Crossan	Damon Curley
Eugene D'Alessandro III	Robert D'Antonio, Jr.	Mark Damato	Daniel DeOrio
Jorge Delgado	William Dempsey, Jr.	Richard Desimone, Jr.	Jeffrey DiPaolo
Michael Donnarumma	John E. Dorman	Peter M. Ellerbrock	Todd Estabrook

Firefighters

Firefighters

Charles E. Ficken

Michael Flood

Daniel Fresse

James Furlong

Frank Gallagher

Glen Gavin

Mitchell D. Gerrity

Vito Gigante

Joseph Gobin

Richard J. Gora

Samuel Griglio

Jose Gutierrez

Steven Haemmerle

Thomas Haemmerle

James R. Halpin

Carlos Hernandez

Firefighters

Steven Hillis	Ruben Hislop	Jason Hodge	John F. Hone
Matthew Huelbig	Thomas Huelbig	Alec Indri	Steven P. Irving
Jose Izquierdo	Kevin Jackson	Robert Jones, Jr.	Christian Jorquera
Gregory Kemp	Louis Knoetig	Mark J. Koenig	William Krieger

Firefighters

Firefighters

Thomas Kross

David Lacarubba

Edward Leao

Frederick Leaycraft

Ramon Leon

Daniel Liberti

Angelo M. Licini

James Lisa

Marc Lombardo

Paul Lopez

Michael Lordo

Anthony Lucia

James H. Maher

Alexander Majors

Thomas J. Malik

Peter Mancini

Firefighters

Dominick Marino	 Francisco D. Martinez	 Michael Mastellone	 Nick Mathioudakis
 Brian T. McCann	 Daniel McEldowney	 Joseph D. McLean III	 Luis Melendez
 Gary V. Mennitto	 Keith G. Mezzina	 Glen S. Michelin	 Raul Mier
 Brian Miller	 Nicola Mitarotonda, Jr.	 John Moore	 Luis F. Morales

Firefighters

Firefighters

Scott T. Morrison	Eugene R. Munafo	Richard Nichols	Gianni Notaro
Salvatore Notaro	Brian T. Notre	Michael Novembre	Roberto Ortiz
John Pachon	Robert Palmer	David E. Pearce	Elvis Pena
Rafael Peralta	John R. Percuoco	Alain Perez	Carlos Perez

Firefighters 89

Firefighters

Nicholas Prato	 Alider Pratts	 Kevin Presutti	 Thomas Primak
 George G. Prina	 Richard A. Prisco	 Adrian Prunes	 Jose Pujols
 Edward B. Quinn	 Anthony Racioppi	 Jose Ramos	 Brian Raparelli
 William R. Reed	 Markus Rehfeld	 William Renner Retired 03-01-09	 Anthony J. Reo

Firefighters

Jeffrey T. Richards

Timothy Richards

Jack Rizzo

Joseph J. Rovito

Henry Ruiz

Albert Salvesen

Thomas Schwartz

Robert Scura

William Sharp, Jr.

Thomas M. Sharples

William Shelton

Terence C. Shevlin

Jason Sibani

Chris M. Sissick

Charles Snyder

Stuart M. Soimes

Firefighters

Brian G. Stahl	 Thomas Steinel	 William Stolc	 Brian Testino
 Glenn W. Teta	 Kevin M. Todd	 John Toomey	 Robert Torres, Jr.
 Orlando Trujillo	 Glenn F. Turner	 Vincent Vacca	 Drew D. Vagts
 Eduardo Valdivia	 Raymond Valenzuela	 Victor Valentin, Jr.	 Thomas G. Van Leuven

Firefighters

Firefighters

Alfredo Vargas, Jr.	Jose A. Vargas	Stefan S. Vassallo	Nicholas Vasta
Richie Velez	Brent Ventura	Mihail E. Voicu	Richard P. Wefer
Edward Wengerter, Jr.	William G. Willard *Retired 08-31-2009*	Thomas Willbergh	Alan William, Jr.
	Erik Wilson	Steven Wojtowicz	

Firefighters 93

Headquarters Staff

Michael DeOrio
Director of Administration

Jeffery Welz
Director of Operations

Linda DiPaolo
Office Manager

Theodora Kross
Accountant

Kimberley Kingsbury
Receptionist

Sonia Pabon
Receptionist

Giovanni D. Ahmad
Computer Service Technician

Michael Dabal
Headquarters Maintenance

Louis Vacca
Building Maintenance

Fire Control

Andrew Scott
Director of Communications

Group A

Noreen Mimi Jones
Supervisor

Frank Silvero

Jennifer Laverty

Group B

Deborah Peek
Supervisor

Laura Roque

Michael Lacenere

Group C

William Miller
Supervisor

Rodolfo Zerquera

Group D

Richard Grome
Supervisor

Juan Borbon

Fire Control 95

Repair & Transportation

Pete Guinchini
Director of Automotives

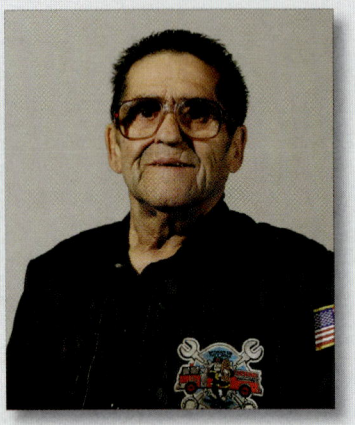

John Ambrosino

Frank Baer

Mercedes Columbie

Orlando Duque

Gary Finkeldey

Tim Firtion

John Hickey

John Lombardi

Denise Mohr

Daniel Peschetti

Steve Peschetti

Michael Smayda

Johnathan Veltre

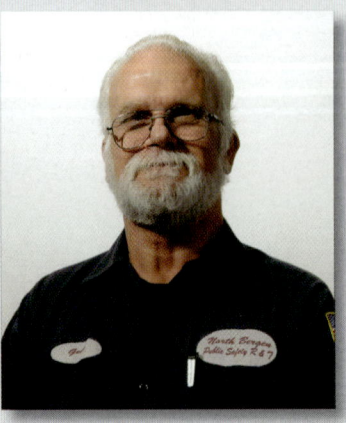

Eugene Watson

Joanne Zoetjes

Repair & Transportation

Retirees

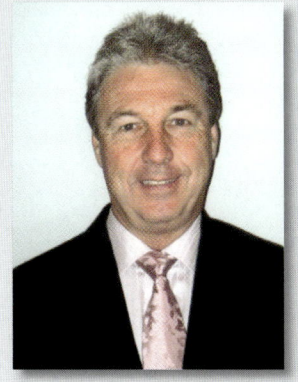

George Aurthur	 Anthony Baglino	 Francis Baker Sr.	 Richard Barreres Sr.	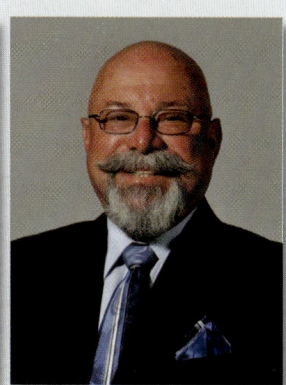 Gustavo A. Baxes
 James Bender	 Angelo Caliente	 Robert "Ace" Cannon	 Michael Collette	 Robert D'Antonio Sr.
 David Denzler	 James Dilworth	 John Eckrote	 Robert Ellerbrock	 Edward Flood
 Carmen T. Galese	 James Hodge	 Robert Hodge	 Eric Inauen	 Gary J. Ippolito

Retirees

Juan Jauregui  | Robert Jones, Sr.  | Ken Kandrac  | John Knoetig  | Joseph Lavelle

Martin J. Mandell  | Ralph Mastellone  | James McLellan  | James McMains  | John Montagne

Robert Montagne  | Kevin Moore  | Richard Paczkowski 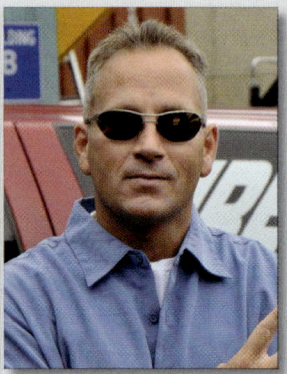 | Nicholas Pallotta  | George Pfeifer

George Pizzuta, Jr.  | Patrick Pizzuta  | Anthony J. Presutti  | Frank Pucher  | Joseph Quigley

Retirees

Retirees

William Renner  • Louis Saber  • Charles Severino  • Michael Smayda  • Gary Stoch Stanke

Charles Steinel  • Robert Taormina  • Ronald Tholen  • Ron Tompkins  • David Velez

Daniel Viscardo, Jr.

Retirees Not Pictured

Rudolph S. Antoncich
Michael P. Ardito
Robert Baldino
Victor Barone
George Brander
George Browne
Robert Cabral
Michael Caliente
Brian C. Canetti
Steven Chrissakis
Robert A. Ciavatta
Christopher J. Crispino
Angelo Defina
Harold Falk
Raymond Ficken
Robert L. Focht
George A. Franke, Jr.
John Gallagher
Steven J. Gibb
Harold J. Granata, Jr.
Albert P. Guzzo
Walter Hanford
Arthur Heydorn

Thomas Hoover
Luke Incognito
Leonard Inzerillo
John A. Kelly
Thomas E. Kelly
Steven Kovacs
Joseph Kritsky
Markos Markou
Alexander Martinez
Calvin Miller
Steven Mirabelli
Alfred R. Mitchell
John Montagne
Kevin J. Moore
David Palmer
John Palombini
Ivan Perez
John Pieretti
John E. Porta
Richard V. Preciose
Alan R. Prellberg
Joseph G. Quigley
Daniel Repetti

Donald J. Ritchie
Robert L. Romano
Domenico Ruocco
John Schriever
Robert Sisserson
Robert W. Stewart
Thomas Teta
Robert Tierney
James Tolomeo
Emil L. Valente
Edward Wengerter
Donald A. Williamson
George L. Zahn
Joseph Zavardino

Deceased Retirees

Rafael Deleon
Ronald Mellifiore
Paul Peters
Dennis St. James
Bruce Tubby
Bruce Wilson

NHRFR
10
SQUAD

NORTH HUDSON
REGIONAL
FIRE RESCUE

North Hudson Regional Fire & Rescue
Fire Companies & Units

A smokey 3-alarm fire on Meadowview Avenue, North Bergen.

Engine Company #1
912 Patterson Plank Road

(Formerly North Bergen Engine Company #2)

Engine 1
1993 Pierce Dash
1500GPM, 750 Tank
(Ex-North Bergen Engine 2)

Quarters of Engine #1.

Engine #1 1993 Pierce

102 North Hudson Regional Fire & Rescue Fire Companies & Units

Squad #2
Quarters

Squad Company #2
1600 New York Avenue, Union City

(Formerly Engine Company #2 North Hudson
Formerly Engine Company #1, Truck 1, Deputy Chief, Fire Headquarters, Fire Alarm and Repair Division)

Squad 2
2005 Pierce Enforcer
1500GPM, 500 Tank
Former Engine 5

Squad 2
1989 Mack CF/Ward 79
1500GPM, 500 Tank
Former Engine 2

Engine 2
1989 Mack CF/Ward 79
1500GPM, 500 Tank
Ex-Union City Engine 1

(Engine 2 re-organized as Squad 2 on March 4, 2004, Special Order 007-04)

Squad #2
2005 Pierce

Squad #2
1989 Mack CF

Engine #2
1989 Mack

North Hudson Regional Fire & Rescue Fire Companies & Units 103

Engine #3 Quarters

Engine #3 Former Quarters

Engine #3 1990 Seagrave

Engine #3 1995 Seagrave

Engine Company #3 & Marine Division
1900 Willow Avenue, Weehawken

(Formerly Truck #2 North Hudson Formerly Weehawken Engine Company #1/Truck #1)

Engine 3
1990 Seagrave
1250GPM, 500 Tank
50ft Squirt
(Former Engine 4 Ex-Weehawken Engine 1 & 2)

Engine 3
1995 Seagrave
1250GPM, 500 Tank
(Ex-Weehawken Engine 3)

(Engine 3 former quarters was located at 133 Jane Street, Weehawken, from January 1999 to November 2002. Former Weehawken Engine 2/1 Quarters)

North Hudson Regional Fire & Rescue Fire Companies & Units

Engine Company #4
541 29th Street, Union City

(Formerly Union City Engine Company's #3, #5, Truck #2, Rescue 1 and Battalion Chief)

Engine 4
1995 Seagrave
1250GPM, 500 Tank
Former Engine 3
(Ex-Weehawken Engine 3)

Engine 4
1990 Seagrave
1250GPM, 500 Tank
50ft Squirt
(Ex-Weehawken Engine 1 & 2)

Engine #4 1995 Seagrave

Engine #4 1990 Seagrave

Engine #4 Quarters

North Hudson Regional Fire & Rescue Fire Companies & Units 105

Engine Company #5
419 43rd Street, Union City

(Formerly Union City Engine Company #4, Truck 3)

New Engine 5 Quarters at 4300 Kennedy Boulevard, Union City, to Open in 2010

Engine 5
2008 Pierce Impels
1500GPM, 500 Tank

Engine 5
2005 Pierce Enforcer
1500GPM, 500 Tank
(Apparatus never assigned due to weight restrictions of quarters reassigned to Squad 2)

Engine 5
1989 Mack CF/Ward 79
1500GPM, 500 Tank
(Ex-Union City Engine 5)

Engine #5 2008 Pierce Impels

Engine #5 2005 Pierce Enforcer

Engine #5 1989 Mack

106 North Hudson Regional Fire & Rescue Fire Companies & Units

Squad #6 2008 Pierce

Squad #6 1988 Spartan Grumman

Squad Company #6
1814 43rd Street, North Bergen

(Formerly North Hudson Engine Company #6 Formerly North Bergen Engine Company #3, Truck #2)

Squad 6
2008 Pierce Impels
1750GPM, 500 Tank
50ft Squirt

Squad 6
1988 Spartan Grumman
1250GPM, 500 Tank
50ft Squirt
(Ex-North Bergen Engine 3)

Engine 6
1988 Spartan Grumman
1250GPM, 500 Tank
50ft Squirt
(Ex-North Bergen Engine 3)

(Engine 6 disbanded to establish Squad 6, August 2, 2007, Special Order 015-04)

Engine #6 1988 Spartan Grumman

North Hudson Regional Fire & Rescue Fire Companies & Units

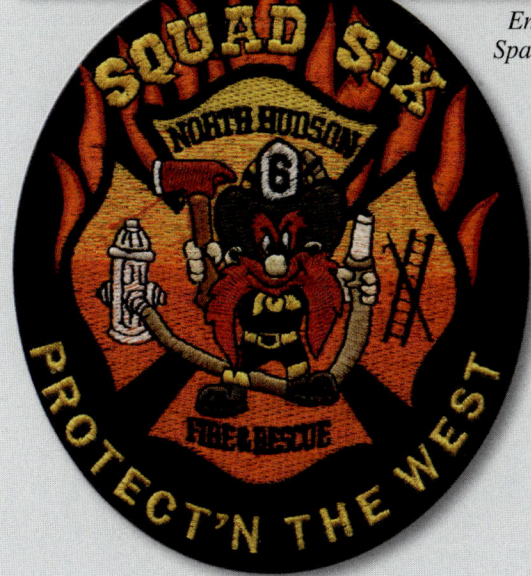

Squad Company #7 & Fire Headquarters

11 Port Imperial Boulevard, West New York

Squad 7
1988 Spartan Grumman
1250GPM, 500 Tank
50ft Squirt
[Former Squad 6]

Squad 7
1993 E-One Cyclone
1500GPM, 750 Tank
[Former Squad 1]
[Former Engine 8]
(Ex-West New York Engine 4)

Squad 7
1994 E-One
1250GPM, 1000 Tank
Top Mount Pump
[Former Engine 12]
(Ex-Guttenberg Engine 1)

Squad 7
1984 Mack MC
1500GPM, 500 Tank
(Ex-Guttenberg Engine 1 & 2. Last All-Mack Pumper ever built. Never assigned to SQ 7)

(Engine 12 disbanded to established Squad 7 at new Fire Headquarters, January 4, 2005, Special Order 015-04)

1988 Spartan Grumman

1993 E-One Cyclone

1994 E-One

Squad #7 1984 Mack MC

Squad #7 Quarters

108 North Hudson Regional Fire & Rescue Fire Companies & Units

Squad #1 2005 Pierce

Squad #1 1993 E-One

Engine #8 1993 E-One

Squad Company #1, Battalion #2 & Fire Control
4911 Broadway, West New York

(Formerly North Hudson Engine Company #8 Formerly West New York Engine Company #4)

Squad 1
2005 Pierce Enforcer
1500GPM, 500 Tank

Squad 1
1993 E-One Cyclone
1500GPM, 750 Tank
(Former Engine 8, Ex-West New York Engine 4)

Engine 8
1993 E-One Cyclone
1500GPM, 750 Tank
(Ex-West New York Engine 4)

(Engine 8 disbanded to establish Squad 1 in March, 2001)

Squad #1 Quarters

North Hudson Regional Fire & Rescue Fire Companies & Units 109

Engine #9 1991 Pierce Dash

Engine Company #9 & Battalion #3
6237 Kennedy Boulevard, North Bergen

(Formerly North Bergen Engine Company #1 And Deputy/Battalion Chief)

Engine 9
1991 Pierce Dash
1500GPM, 750 Tank
(Ex-North Bergen Engine 1)

110 | North Hudson Regional Fire & Rescue Fire Companies & Units

Squad Company #10
6510 Hudson Avenue, West New York

(Formerly North Hudson Engine Company #10 Formerly West New York Engine Company #3/Truck #2/Engine Company #6)

Squad #10 1993 E-One

Squad 10
1993 E-One
1500GPM, 750 Tank
(Former Squad 1, 7, Former Engine 8, Ex-West New York Engine 4)

Squad #10 2001 American LaFrance

Squad 10
2001 American LaFrance
2000 GPM 950 Tank 50 gal. foam
Rescue Pumper
*(Ex Voorhees (NJ) Engine 6031
Leased as temporary replacement
for totaled apparatus.)*

Squad #10 1987 Spartan Grumman

Squad 10
1987 Spartan Grumman
1250GPM, 750 Tank
(Former Engine 14, Ex-West New York Engine 3)

Squad #10 1993 E-One

Squad 10
1993 E-One Cyclone
1500GPM, 750 Tank
*(Ex-West New York Engine 5
Totaled in MVA January 2008)*

Engine 10
1993 E-One Cyclone
1500GPM, 750 Tank
(Ex-West New York Engine 5)

(Engine 10 disbanded to establish Squad 10, February 3, 2004, Special Order 003-04)

Engine #10 1993 E-One Cyclone

North Hudson Regional Fire & Rescue Fire Companies & Units

Squad #10 Quarters

Engine Company #11

580 66th Street, West New York

(Formerly West New Engine Company #6/Truck #2)

Engine 11
1988 Spartan Grumman
1250GPM, 750 Tank
50ft Squirt
(Ex-North Bergen Engine 2, 5)

Engine #11 1988 Spartan Grumman

North Hudson Regional Fire & Rescue Fire Companies & Units 113

Engine Company #13
7507 Hudson Avenue, North Bergen

(Formerly North Bergen Engine Company #4)

Engine 13
1993 Pierce Dash
1500GPM, 750 Tank

Engine #13 1993 Pierce Dash

114 North Hudson Regional Fire & Rescue Fire Companies & Units

Ladder #1 Quarters

Ladder #1 2008 Pierce Arrow XT

Ladder #1 1985/1986 Seagrave 100 ft Tiller

Ladder #1 Frankenstein

Ladder Company #1
1600 New York Avenue, Union City

(Formerly Union City Truck #1)

Ladder 1
2008 Pierce Arrow XT
100 Ft. Tiller

Ladder 1
1985/1986 Seagrave
100 ft Tiller
*(Ex-Ladder 4 Cab
Ex-Ladder 1, 7, 2, 9 Trailer)*

North Hudson Regional Fire & Rescue Fire Companies & Units 115

Ladder 1
1985 Seagrave
100ft Tiller
(*Former Ladder 4, Ex-West New York Truck 1*)

Ladder 1
1986 Seagrave
100ft Tiller
(*Ex-Union City L-1*)

Ladder 1
1988 Pierce
105ft Tiller
(*Former Ladder 9, Ex-North Bergen L-2, Ex-Pittsburgh, PA L-1*)

Ladder #1 1985 Seagrave

Ladder #1 1986 Seagrave

Ladder #1 1988 Pierce

116 **North Hudson Regional Fire & Rescue Fire Companies & Units**

Ladder #2 Quarters

Ladder Company #2
541 29th Street, Union City

(Formerly Union City Truck #2)

Ladder 2
2005 Pierce Dash
100ft Tiller

Ladder 2
1986 Seagrave
100ft Tiller Former Ladder 1, 7
(Ex-Union City Ladder 1)

Ladder 2
1990 Seagrave Rearmount Quint
1250GPM, 500 Tank
(Ex-Weehawken Truck 1)

Ladder #2 2005 Pierce Dash

Ladder #2 1986 Seagrave

Ladder #2 1990 Seagrave Rearmount Quint

North Hudson Regional Fire & Rescue Fire Companies & Units 117

Ladder Company 3
4610 Park Avenue, Weehawken

(Formerly North Hudson Ladder #3 & Rescue 1
Formerly Weehawken Engine
Company 3 & Truck #2
And Weehawken Fire Headquaters)

Ladder 3
1995 Seagrave
100ft Rearmount
(Ex-Weehawken Ladder 3)

Ladder #3 1995 Seagrave

118 **North Hudson Regional Fire & Rescue Fire Companies & Units**

Ladder #4 2003 Pierce Dash

Ladder Company 4
428 60th Street, West New York

(Formerly West New York Truck #1, Deputy/Battalion West New York Fire Headquarters and Fire Alarm)

Ladder 4
2003 Pierce Dash
100ft Tiller

Ladder 4
1985 Seagrave
100ft. Tiller
(Ex-West New York Truck 1)

Ladder #4 Quarters

Ladder #4 1985 Seagrave

North Hudson Regional Fire & Rescue Fire Companies & Units

Ladder Company #5
8311 Kennedy Boulevard, North Bergen

(Formerly North Bergen Truck#1)

Ladder 5
2005 Pierce Dash
100ft Tiller

Ladder 5
1986 Maxim
100ft Tiller
(Ex-North Bergen Truck 1)

Ladder #5 2005 Pierce Dash

Ladder #5 1986 Maxim

Ladder #5 Quarters

120 **North Hudson Regional Fire & Rescue Fire Companies & Units**

Engine #4, Ladder #2 and Deputy #1

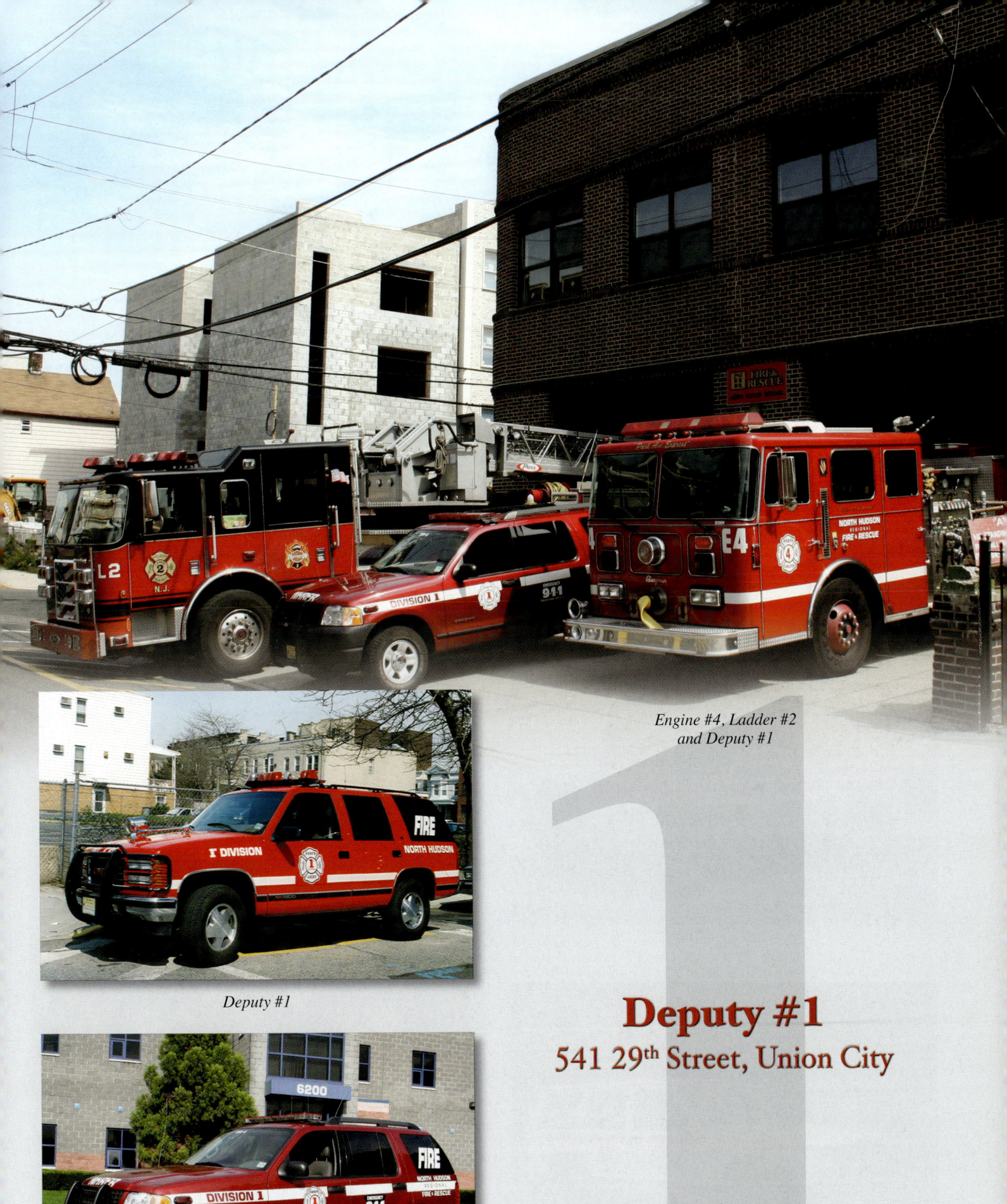

Deputy #1

Deputy #1

Deputy #1
541 29th Street, Union City

North Hudson Regional Fire & Rescue Fire Companies & Units 121

Battalion #1 Quarters

Battalion #1

Battalion #1

Battalion #1

Battalion 1
1600 New York Avenue, Union City

122 North Hudson Regional Fire & Rescue Fire Companies & Units

Battalion 2
4911 Broadway, West New York

Battalion #2

Battalion #2

Battalion 3
6237 Kennedy Boulevard, North Bergen

Battalion #3 Quarters

Battalion #3

North Hudson Regional Fire & Rescue Fire Companies & Units

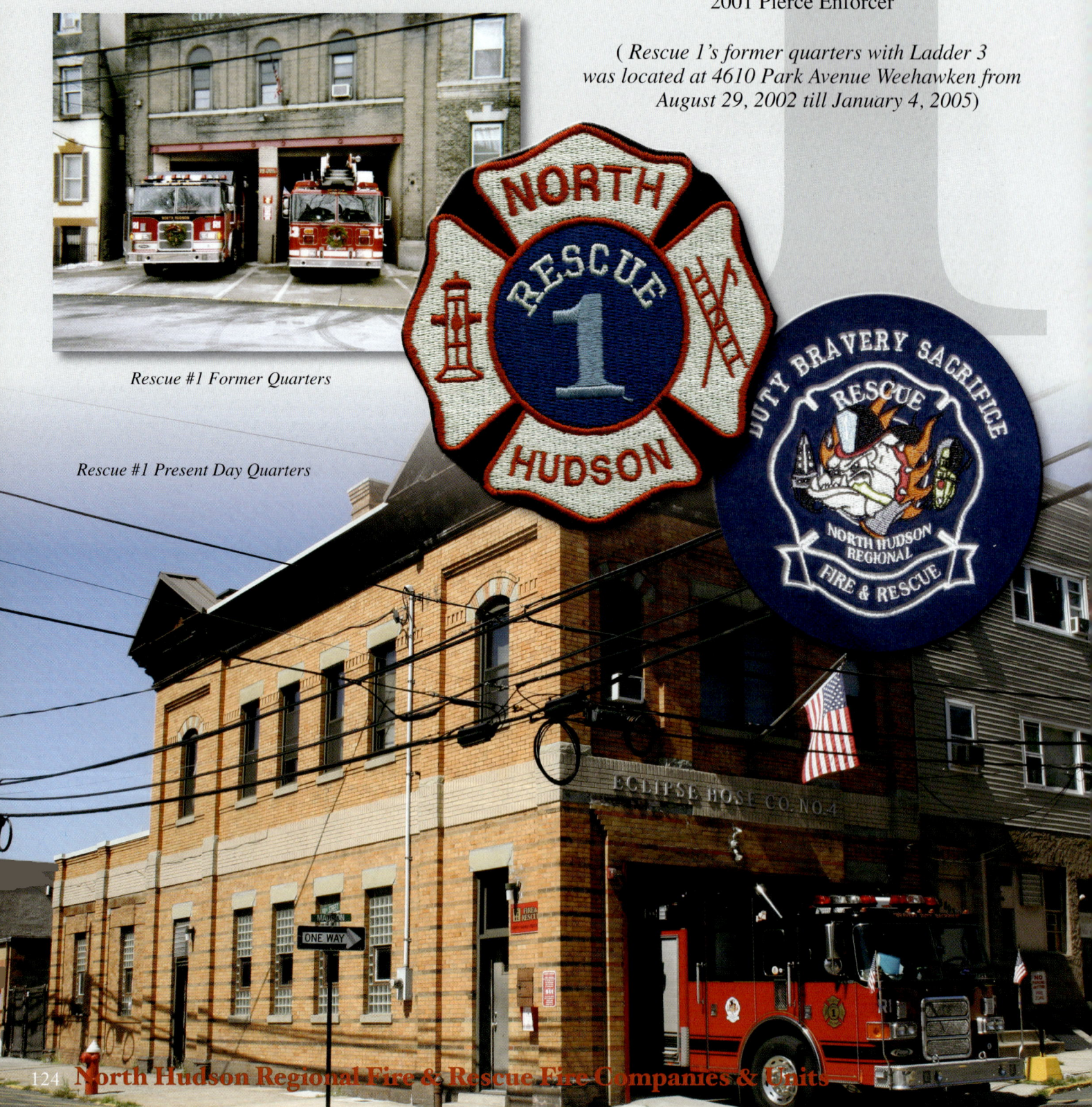

Rescue Company #1
6801 Madison Avenue, Guttenberg

Formerly North Hudson Engine Company #12
Formerly Guttenberg Engine Company #1
(career) And Eclipse Hose
Company #4 (Volunteer)

Rescue 1
2001 Pierce Enforcer

(*Rescue 1's former quarters with Ladder 3 was located at 4610 Park Avenue Weehawken from August 29, 2002 till January 4, 2005)*

Rescue #1 2001 Pierce Enforcer

Rescue #1 Former Quarters

Rescue #1 Present Day Quarters

124 North Hudson Regional Fire & Rescue Fire Companies & Units

Rescue Company #1

In November 2000, North Hudson Regional Fire and Rescue, after a thorough analysis, decided to implement a technical rescue company.

The need was largely due to the intense demographics of the five cities that regionalized to form one department. The area is one of the most densely populated in the United States. It includes a major commuting hub into New York City, including major highways, the Lincoln Tunnel, Amtrak tunnels into Manhattan, the Hudson-Bergen Light Rail, the cliffs on the Palisades, numerous houses of worship for multiple ethnicities, and the NY Waterway Ferry service that operates on the Hudson River. The daytime population is also larger because of numerous office buildings and warehouse complexes. Due to the close proximity to New York City, the terrorist threat is always high.

Chief of Department Edward Flood formed the committee, which included Battalion Chief Frank Montagne (now Deputy Chief), Captain Anthony Venezia, and Firefighter Robert P. Morrison III (now Captain.)

The committee was responsible for researching all areas of technical rescue, including High Angle, Confined Space, Auto Extrication, Building Collapse, Tools and Equipment, and any other technical rescue beyond normal firefighting duties. The committee members sought information from surrounding departments and other large departments in the Northeast. They gathered information regarded Standard Operating Procedures (SOP), Company Policy, Running Assignments, Tool Specifications, Training SOP, Vendors for Training, Bids for Tools and Equipment, and Apparatus Specification and Design.

In December 2000, the committee expanded to include three more Captains as new Rescue officers: Captains Richard Barreres, Michael Hern, and David Flood. The committee also added two firefighters: William Reed and Sean Miick (now Captain.)

In January 2001, the Department transferred all prospective members to 1600 New York Avenue in Union City – Ladder Company 1 – to start training for this special operations company. Ladder 1 was an appropriate ladder due to its numerous storage capabilities for the large amounts of equipment being purchased.

At this time, the members were receiving and training extensively on the new tools that were purchased for this special operations company. The members sought permission to train on vacant buildings, properties under renovation, and wherever else they could further their knowledge on the extensive amount of equipment being purchased.

Outside vendors for training and vendors for the newly purchased equipment were actively training the newly formed rescue crews. This type of special operations training still continues on a daily basis.

After months of extensive training, the Rescue Company was formally put into service in August 2002. The new apparatus was a 2001 Pierce Enforcer. The company was stationed in the most centrally located house in the region, at 4610 Park Avenue, Weehawken, with Ladder Company 3.

The running assignments for the department were changed to accommodate Rescue Company 1. The new company's response consisted of Structure Fires, Vehicle Extrications, Technical Rescues, Bomb Scares, Terrorist Threats, Suspicious Packages, Special Calls at the Incident Commander's Request, and any other situation out of the normal firefighting realm.

The company's highly motivated members even renovated the kitchen at their firehouse to accommodate the eight men per house – the men in Rescue Company 1 and Ladder Company 3. This was also an appropriate time to start cross training with the members of Ladder Company 3.

Shortly thereafter, a rescue task force was formed consisting of Squad Company 1, Squad Company 10, Ladder Company 3 and Ladder Company 4. These additional members were vital for completing all functions of a technical rescue, due to the complex, unique, and manpower-intensive operations. These members were also utilized to provide trained personnel for back-up rescue personnel.

The Rescue Company went to work right away, performing such rescues as Trench Rescues, Building Collapses, Vehicles into Buildings, Industrial Accidents, High Angle Rescues, and numerous Vehicle Extrication Rescues, on top of their normal structural firefighting duties.

In coming years, the rescue company will also perform more complex rescues, such as if a commercial jet liner goes down in the Hudson River, light rail accidents involving commuter buses – the list goes on.

In 2004, a grant was given to the State of New Jersey to form an Urban Area Security Initiative (UASI). This grant was formed through the United States Department of Homeland Security to increase the state's capabilities to combat any other terrorist actions or major catastrophes. North Hudson was chosen as one of the nine UASI response teams, which were trained together by New Jersey Task Force One Urban Search and Rescue Team.

The UASI grant provided all nine teams with a Spartan P.L. custom rescue apparatus. This apparatus was received in 2006 and is assigned as North Hudson Rescue Company 2. Each team was also given identical tool caches. North Hudson is now responsible for responding throughout the state for any major technical rescue at the request of the N.J. State Police. There have been several state responses since this task force was formed, including a building collapse in Irvington, a high-rise collapse in Paterson, a car into building in Garfield, and more in time.

In January 2005, Rescue 1 was relocated to a new firehouse at 6801 Madison Street in Guttenberg. This was due to the closing of Engine 12, to place in service the newly formed Squad 7. Squad 7 was assigned to 11 Port Imperial Boulevard in West New York. This firehouse also serves as Fire Headquarters.

Due to manpower shortages and budget constraints, in July 2009 Rescue Company 1 was added to a list for rotational firehouse closings. These closings caused Rescue Company 1 to be reassigned to a special call apparatus. The members were reassigned to Squad Company 6.

Rescue Company 1 was relocated to 1813 44th Street in North Bergen, Squad Company 6. Rescue Company 1 is in service responding to normal assignments when manpower permits.

Charter members of Rescue Company 1 formally placed in service in August 2002

Chief of Special Operations: Battalion Chief Frank Montagne

1st Platoon	2nd Platoon	3rd Platoon	4th Platoon
Captain	**Captain**	**Captain**	**Captain**
Richard Barreres	Anthony Venezia	Michael Hern	David Flood
Firefighters	**Firefighters**	**Firefighters**	**Firefighters**
Gregory Kemp	Robert Morrison	Brian Cosentino	Gary Mennitto
Keith Mezzina	John Dorman	Richard Gora	Pete Mancini
Luis Melendez	William Reed	Leonel Calvo	Scott Marione

(Submitted by: Captain Anthony Venezia, Captain Robert Morrison, and Firefighter William Reed)

Rescue Company #2/U.A.S.I.

11 Port Imperial Boulevard, West New York

The New Jersey Metro Urban Search and Rescue (USAR) Strike Team was submitted on February 1, 2004. Through Federal, funding and local planning two USAR Strike Teams were formed on July 31, 2006. They are comprised of nine municipal Fire Department Rescue Companies and the Port Authority of New York and New Jersey's Emergency Services Unit. The Fire Departments that comprise the USAR Strike Teams are Newark, Jersey City, Bayonne, Hoboken, North Hudson Regional, Elizabeth, Hackensack, Paterson, and Morristown. The Rescue Companies from these departments will form a mutual aid resource team from which assets can be drawn to organize a highly trained and equipped first response urban search and rescue capability. The ten departments are capable of forming two USAR Strike Teams.

A Strike Team can be activated by any of the ten member departments, the County Fire Coordinator of any of the six Urban Area Security Initiative (UASI) counties, the State's Regional Fire Coordinator, State's Fire Marshal, or the Governor of the State of New Jersey. Whenever a Metro USAR Strike Team is activated, New Jersey's USAR-Task Force 1 will be notified. The USAR Strike Teams will individually be under the command of a Strike Team Leader, who will report to the appropriate supervisor as prescribed by the National Incident Management System (NIMS) protocols. Metro USAR Strike Team responses conform to the local and regional mutual aid agreements as well as State of New Jersey legal requirements.

Metro USAR Strike Teams provide a means to rapidly provide a highly qualified and professional Urban Search and Rescue response to any large-scale structural collapse disaster as well as related incidents that require technical rescue capabilities in order to save lives and reduce property loss. By providing appropriate and standardized equipment along with the required training, the ten participating departments in this initiative will be able to coordinate their efforts into teams.

These Strike Teams greatly enhance the regions ability to respond effectively to natural and manmade disasters. Additionally the USAR Strike Teams represent a coordinated mutual aid effort between the nine municipal Fire Departments, the Port Authority of NY & NJ and the New Jersey State's Urban Search and Rescue Task Force One and as such increase the continuity between local and state resources during major incidents that outstrip a local regions capability. Individual Rescue Companies that make up the Strike Teams will also be used locally to enhance the rescue capabilities on a daily basis in their communities.

Submitted by Deputy Chief Frank Montagne, Metro Strike Team Chairman

Marine Company 1

1900 Willow Avenue, Weehawken

Soon after the inception of the North Hudson Regional Fire and Rescue in 1999, the need for a Marine company was talked about due to the amount of waterfront now included in the department. The waterfront included marinas, waterfront restaurants, condominium developments, the New York Waterways main ferry terminal, Hudson River walkway, as well as parks and playgrounds which draw many people to the waters edge.

The Hudson River in its self is a very busy waterway with both commercial and pleasure craft plying the waterway, sightseeing helicopter tours, dinner cruise ships, sightseeing boat tours, sailboats, right down to wave runners and kayakers. If it floats rest assure you will see it on the river.

Our first boat was a 16 ft. fiberglass boat donated by a department member; this was barely adequate for our growing needs. Our second boat came from Stony Point, New York. Shamrock Boat Builders built this 28 ft. 1986 fiberglass boat for the Stony Point Fire Department. She was powered by a V-8 Ford Marine Engine inboard with a full keel. After the Department purchased it, she was trailered to Engine 3's quarters, where she was blocked up, stripped down, and rewired. New electronics were installed, as well new lettering and a fresh coat of paint top and bottom. A Hale 550 GPM pump mounted in the bow which is connected to a deck gun mounted on the bow, and 2–1¾ discharge outlets for hand line operations. Our boat drafts 30", which allows us to operate in shallow water near the shore line. Marine 1 is docked at Lincoln Harbor Yacht Club in Weehawken and is manned by the crew of Engine Company 3. The firehouse is located only 5-6 minutes from the marina and can be underway in 6-8 minutes.

Since the purchase of our second Marine 1, she has seen action in the Hackensack River in Kearny for a pier fire, and the offshore power boat races that are held in the Hudson River where a large powerboat broke apart after becoming air born, hitting the water and breaking apart. The boat sunk leaving its five crew members in the water, without life jackets. Marine 1 along with a private boat, pulled the injured crew out and transported them to the Edgewater Marina on the New Jersey side for medical attention. The next incident was when a tourist helicopter lost power and crash landed in Weehawken by Arthur's Landing in the river while escorting the famous Word War II carrier U.S.S. *Intrepid* to Bayonne New Jersey for a two-year overhaul. Once again, we found ourselves in need of a larger vessel that can be keep in the water year round, and be able to carry more equipment and man power as well as take what mother nature can throw at us.

During the winter of 2004, word of a 32 ft. patrol boat that the N.J.S.P. used was going on the auction block, so the push to acquire it began. For the next two years a lot of phone calls, leg work and sea trials and to show the need for a larger vessel began. When it went up for auction, the Department bid on and won the purchase of our current Marine 1. This vessel is a 32 ft. all aluminum patrol boat with a 11' 6" beam powered by Twin V6-53 Detroit Diesel engines. Unique for this boat is it has tunnel drive, which means the props are tucked up in the hull with only one blade of the prop below the keel. This protects the props from damage. Both engines were rebuilt by the State of New Jersey in 2003 with only 500 hours on the motors and transmission. On December 29, 2006, Marine 1 was sailed up to Lincoln Harbor Marina from Point Pleasant, N.J. arrangements were made for the transportation of Marine 1 to the quarters of Engine 3 where for a second time E-3 crew was again given the task of transforming this police boat into a fully functional fire/rescue boat.

For the next seven months she was totally stripped down inside and out, the cabin was fully rewired, insulated, air conditioner unit installed, new upholstery, the latest electronics UHF and Department radios GPS and radar, as well as high intensity lighting for night ops. A 550 GPM Hale pump was mounted on the rear deck, port side, piped up from the bottom of the boat, to the pump, then back below deck, threw the engine room up to the bow to the remote controlled deck gun mounted on the bow, which is controlled from the safety of the cabin, the pump also has 2-1¾ outlets for hand lines to be used from the deck. The starboard side has a 3kw Honda generator that supplies power to the cabin air conditioning & high-intensity telescoping flood light on the rear deck.

The hull was stripped down to the bare metal primed and three coats of fire engine red were applied above the waterline for its glossy shine. The cabin was done in glossy white, the handrails done in glossy red; deck is done tan with a non-skid finish. To finish it off the lettering would give it the final touch. While all of the work was going on, our Department suffered a tragic loss of one of our own. On September 9, 2006, Firefighter Vincent Neglia was killed while searching for victims of a fire in Union City. The idea of naming our fireboat after Vincent Neglia was kicked around by the crews of Engine 3, who all agreed this would be a great way to remember our fallen brother. A report was written to the Chief of Department with this idea, who in turn gave the approval to this and now took on a completely new meaning for us in finishing Marine 1. On August 23, 2007, the fireboat *Vincent Neglia* was christened by members of Firefighter Neglia's family at the Lincoln Harbor Marina and was placed into service as the newest piece of firefighting equipment in the Department arsenal. Our former Marine 1 was then sold to the Edgewater Fire Department Edgewater, New Jersey which is adjacent to the northern border of the department jurisdiction.

Marine #1 when it was received.

Marine #1

Marine #1

Marine #1

Marine #1

Training

All crew members that were assigned to Marine 1 completed a Boater Safety Course that is given by the United States Coast Guard and required by law. Next, the New Jersey State Police supplied the Department with a State Trooper from their Marine Division who was stationed on the 32 ft. to do boat handling docking, GPS & radar both day and night time until all crews were signed off on and able to handle Marine 1. The next level of training again given by the State Police was the open-water rescue classes which again built confidence in our boat crews. During the summer months, man overboard drills are preformed in the river with crewmembers, taking turns in the water as victim and other crewmembers to rotate as lookout, pilot and victim as well as donning our survival suits.

Marine 1 has a great working relationship with the United States Coast Guard, the New Jersey State Police. Marine Units, Jersey City's Marine Unit, Edgewater's Marine 1, as well as the New York Police Department Harbor Units and the New York Fire Department Marine Units who all share the common goal of helping our fellow man in his or her time on need.

Patrol Areas

Our patrols run the New Jersey side of the Hudson River up to Alpine, New Jersey down to Newark Bay and up into the Hackensack River in Secaucus, New Jersey. Patrols go for two-three hours both day and night all year round.

On May 31, 2008, a request for Marine 1 to supply escort and a water display in the Hudson for a United States Marine, Sergeant Merlin German who had 97% burns over his body from a roadside bomb in Iraq. He died in 2008 following his 158th surgery, he only had a 3% chance of survival and excruciating pain, German 22, lifted the spirits of other patients and

128 North Hudson Regional Fire & Rescue Fire Companies & Units

started Merlin's Miracles a Foundation similar to Make a Wish. This year the Burn Advocates Group met at the marina for its rally. Friends and family members as well as burn victims rode 15 pedal powered water bikes across the Hudson including one empty bike flying the United States Marine Corp Flag in his honor. The group pedaled past a United States Destroyer where the Marines on board snapped to attention and gave a salute to the group and fallen comrade.

On December 10, 2008, Dispatch received a call of a boat fire in the same marina where Marine 1 is docked. The change of shift was going on at this time and the off going crew said they would operate Marine 1 and the on duty crew would respond with Engine 3. Crews were met with heavy fire and black smoke coming from two large boats tied up on one of the finger piers, with smoke and heat traveling towards shore. Marine 1 was underway and was able to position itself up wind and trained its deck gun and hand lines on the flaming vessels. Marine 1 with the help of the United States Coast Guard who sent a 41 footer and New York Fire Department Marine Unit kept the fire in check while land units were making there way via the floating docks. Both boats and one finger pier received heavy damage with both boats sunk at the dock and area boats received smoke and some water damage.

At 1534 on January 15, 2009, something happened in the Hudson River that no one would believe but a commercial airliner made a perfect landing in the near freezing waters. Marine 1 was dispatched and was one of the first group of rescue vessels on scene and started to look for survivors. As the day progressed, SCUBA teams from New York Fire Department were on board helping with the recovery efforts. Marine 1 was then asked to retrieve all floating debris from the crash and bring to the ferry terminal where the Incident Command center was located. Once again, the *Vincent Neglia* was proven to be a great asset to the Department.

At 1202 on August 8, 2009, a radio alarm was transmitted for Marine 1 to respond to the waters off Hoboken for a reported collision between a plane and sightseeing helicopter. Only this time there were no survivors, Marine 1 started a grid search and retrieved any floating debris then turning it over to the Harbor Units of the New York Police Department at the crash site. This was going to be a long and timely recovery, which stretched into almost six days until all victims were removed from the Hudson. By the end of the day, Marine 1 returned to the dock and all water operations were turned over to the New York Police Department divers and the Army Corps of Engineers who raised both aircraft from the murky Hudson.

Therefore, as long as people are drawn to the waters edge for their pleasure and enjoyment in whatever mode of transport they choose and the need for a marine unit has proven itself time and time again. The *Vincent Neglia* will be ready to respond and give assistance whenever needed no matter what the weather or time of day all year round.

(Submitted by Captain Keith Gonyou, Engine 3/Marine 1)

Marine Division Car #6

Marine Division Quarters

Safety #1 Quarters

Safety #1 1994 Ford Superduty/Cliffside Body Company

Safety #1 & Mask Service Unit

133 Jane Street, Weehawken

(Formerly North Hudson Engine Company #3
Formerly Weehawken Engine Company #2 / 1)

Safety 1
1994 Ford Superduty
6 Bottle Cascade

(Former Quarters were located at
1600 New York Avenue, Union City,
from May 2000 to November 2002)

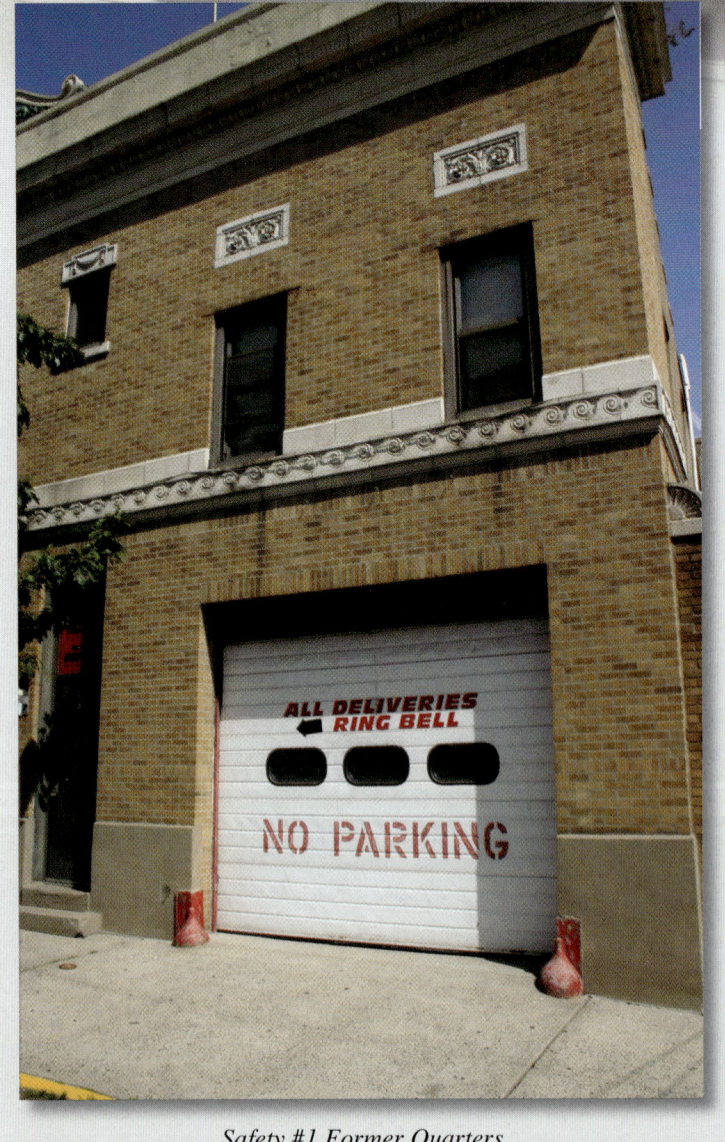

Safety #1 Former Quarters

North Hudson Regional Fire & Rescue Fire Companies & Units

North Hudson Regional Fire & Rescue Safety Officer

One of the best ways to reduce injuries at Fire Department incidents is the appointment of a well prepared, trained Safety Officer. North Hudson Regional Fire & Rescue assigned the position of Safety Officer in May of 2000. All Company Officers, Battalion Chiefs, and Deputy Chiefs received training using National Fire Protection Association (NFPA) Standard 1500,1501 and later Standard 1521: as their guidelines. Before Regionalization the individual Fire Departments did not have a designated full time Safety Officer. The first assigned Safety Officers had their work cut out for them. They had to learn the responsibility of being the Incident Scene Safety Officer and also be in charge of the Occupational Safety and Health Compliance Training. These new Safety Officers did a fantastic job of learning their new job descriptions and implementing the compliance training. Captain Ron Tompkins, (promoted to Battalion Chief retired 2007), Captain Victor "Chuck" Barone, (retired 2007), Captain Michael Cranwell (promoted to Battalion Chief 2002), Captain Richard Preciose (retired 2006), were four of the driving forces that implemented many of these programs to get them up and running. The Department owes them many thanks and their work will always be appreciated.

The Safety Officers when first assigned rode out of the 1600 New York Avenue firehouse. Engine 2, Ladder 1, and Battalion 1 are assigned to this station. At that time the Safety Officer did not have an assigned driver, now called the Command Tech. The vehicle assigned to the Safety Officer was the original North Bergen Mask Service Unit (MSU). This is a 1994 Ford Superduty that carries a six-bottle air cascade system and generator to fill Self Contained Breathing Apparatus (SCBA) air bottles at large scale incidents. The MSU also carries approximately 40 spare SCBA bottles for immediate use. Before regionalization the MSU was requested at mutual aid fires throughout the county to bring additional air to large scale incidents. This vehicle is still in service and maintained by the head of the Repairs and Transportation Department (also called The Shops) Pete Guinchini. A new Safety Officers vehicle has been requested by the Department at the time of this writing. In November 2002, the Safety Officer was reassigned to the Jane Street firehouse in Weehawken.

Starting in July 2009, due to a hiring freeze and lack of manpower, the Department started to close an engine or squad on a rotating basis, and if necessary Rescue 1. On these tours, the Safety Officer will be assigned to Squad 2, Engine 9, Engine 11, or Rescue 1's quarters depending on which companies are closed.

Some of the duties of a North Hudson Regional Fire & Rescue Safety Officer are listed below:

1. Incident scene safety.
2. Record, document and investigate every firefighter injury.
3. Record, document investigate every vehicle accident involving a NHRF&R apparatus.
4. SCBA mask fit test for all members of the department.
5. Replace damaged SCBA harnesses to all companies.
6. Bloodborne pathogen compliance training to all members.
7. Right to Know compliance training to all members.
8. Masked Services Unit training.
9. Replace damaged fireground radios to members.
10. Hazardous Vacant Building marking system.
11. Attend training sessions to oversee safety.

The Comman Technician

In 2002, when the Safety Officer was assigned to ride out of the Jane Street firehouse in Weehawken due to Engine 3 being reassigned to the 19th Street and Willow Avenue firehouse. The Command Technician was created to drive Deputy 1 in 2001, and then was later reassigned to the Safety Officer. The Safety Officer would be the only apparatus riding out of this station. This was also a new position created within the Fire Department. This position was filled by a firefighter who also had to learn his newly assigned duties and responsibilities. Some of the Command Technician assigned duties are:

1. Setting up the Incident Command Board at Fire Department incidents
2. Monitoring radio transmissions on the fireground
3. Accountability and roll call
4. Getting all pertinent information for fire reports and NFIRS.
5. Chauffeur of the MSU- check apparatus daily
6. Spare weekly radio check

The Command Technician is the incident commanders eyes and ears on the fireground. Many of the newly assigned Command Technician's did a great job of learning their responsibilities and helped train other Command Technician's who took their place. Some of the first appointed Command Technician's were, Firefighter John Porta, (retired 2007), Firefighter Alan Cody, (still active), Firefighter Gustavo Baxes, (retired 2007), Firefighter Dominic Sico (promoted to Captain 2006). These first Command Technician's did a great job of learning the importance of this position and being an extension of the Safety Officers.

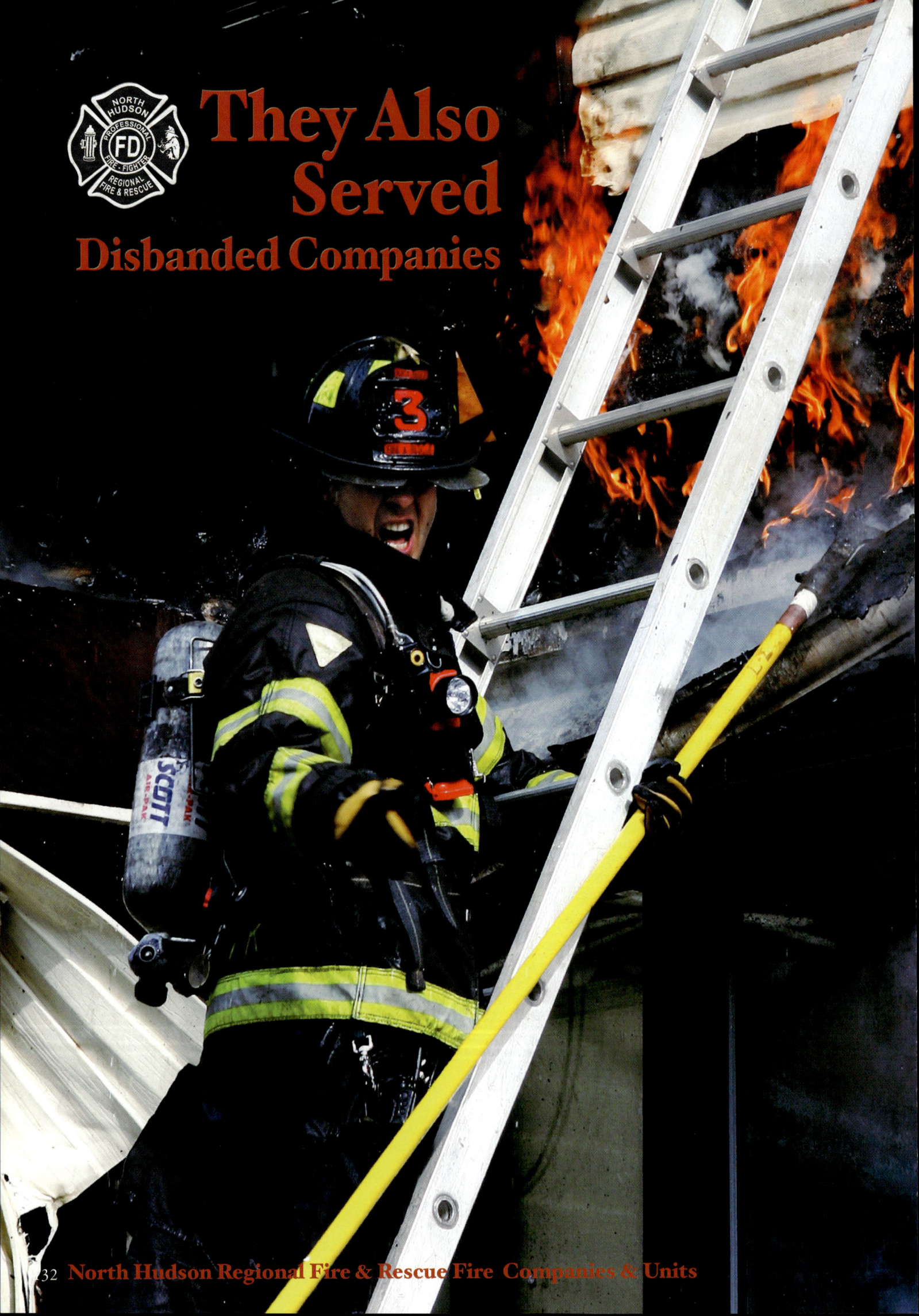

They Also Served
Disbanded Companies

North Hudson Regional Fire & Rescue Fire Companies & Units

Engine Company #7

303 47th Street, Union City

(Formerly Union City Engine Company #6)

Engine 7
1980 Mack CF Refurbished in 1988
(Ex. Union City Engine #3 & #7)

(Disbanded August 29, 2002 to establish Rescue Company #1)

North Hudson Regional Fire & Rescue Fire Companies & Units

They Also Served
Engine Company #12
6801 Madison Street, Guttenberg

(Formerly North Hudson Engine Company #12 & Formerly Guttenberg Engine Company #1)

Engine 12
1994 Emergency One 1250/1000 tank
1st top mounted Pump panel in North Hudson and only single stage pumper.

(Disbanded January 4, 2005 to establish Squad #7)

134   **North Hudson Regional Fire & Rescue Fire Companies & Units**

They Also Served
Engine Company #14
625 61ST Street, West New York

(Formerly West New York Engine Company #5 & Emergency Truck #7)

Engine 14
1986 Spartan/Grumman

(Disbanded July 2000)

They Also Served

Engine Company #15

4800 Avenue at Port Imperial Boulevard, West New York

Established August 5, 2002
Closed May 4, 2003

Engine 15 was established for the purpose of providing fire protection during the construction phase of Pershing Road. Due to it's location, the waterfront became a thriving real estate mecca, with the introduction of hi-rises as well as lo-rise condominiums and town houses. It was proposed by one of the developers to construct a fire house after the first phase of construction was completed.

(The new fire house now houses Squad #7, U.A.S.I. Rescue 2 and Fire Headquarters.)

Car #4

Car #7 Training Division

Car #10

Car #10

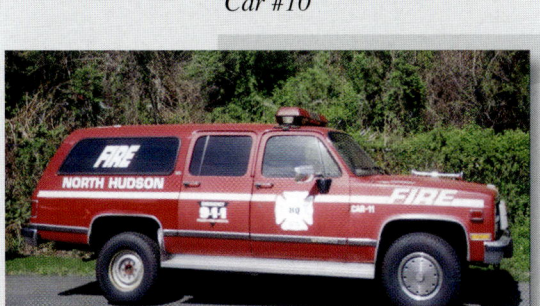

Car #11

Car #14

11 Port Imperial Boulevard

Fire Headquarters

1999 ~ 2005
6000 Tonnelle Avenue Bld. 1

2005 ~ Present
11 Port Imperial Boulevard

Satellite Headquarters
1600 New York Avenue

2005 ~ Present

North Hudson Regional Fire & Rescue Fire Companies & Units 137

Home of Fire Control was opened in 2010.

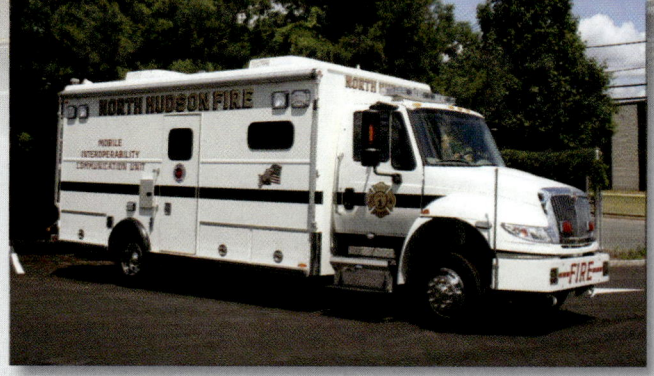

Mobile Interoperability Communication Unit

Home of Fire Control from 1982 to 2010.

Unit 200

Fire Control

1982-2010
4911 Broadway, West New York

Future Home of Fire Control
4300 Kennedy Boulevard, Union City

Unit 200

138 **North Hudson Regional Fire & Rescue Fire Companies & Units**

Engine #14 1986 Spartan/Grumman

Spare/Reserve Apparatus

Engine #14
Formerly West New York Engine 3
1986 Spartan/Grumman

Engine #15
Formerly Union City Engine 5
1986 Mack CF/Ward 79

Engine #16
Formerly Guttenberg Engine 1 &
Hose Company #2
1984 Mack MC
(One of the last "ALL MACK" apparatus ever built)

Engine #16
Formerly Union City Engine 1 &6
1980 Mack/CF

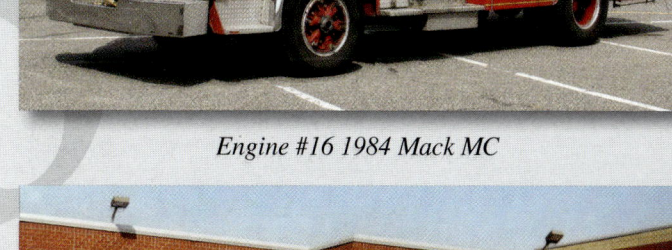

Engine #15 1986 Mack CF/Ward 79

Engine #16 1984 Mack MC

Engine #16 1980 Mack/CF

North Hudson Regional Fire & Rescue Fire Companies & Units

Engine #17 1988 Mack CF/Ward 79

Spare/Reserve Apparatus

Engine #17
Formerly North Hudson Engine 2, Squad 2 and Union City Engine 1
1988 Mack CF/Ward 79

(*This is one of two pumpers delivered to Union City with flow meters, a first for North Hudson area.*)

Engine #17
Formerly North Hudson Engine 7 and Union City Engine 3, Engine 7
1980 Mack CF
(*Refurbished in 1988*)

Engine #17
Formerly Weehawken Engine 1 & Paramus Engine 3
1980 Duplex Great Eastern

(*This apparatus was loaned to Fairview, where it road as engine Company #1, for one year. Upon returning to the regional, it was later donated to the Dominican Republic.*)

Engine #17 1980 Mack CF

Engine #17 1980 Duplex Great Eastern

Engine #18 1994 Emergency One

Spare/Reserve Apparatus

Engine #18
Formerly North Hudson Engine 12, Squad 7, and Guttenberg Engine Company 1/Hose Company 4
1994 Emergency One

(One of the first top mounted pump panels in North Hudson.)

Engine #18
Formerly North Hudson Engine 19 and Union City Engine 4
1986 Mack/Ward 79

(On loan to Jersey City for the months as Engine #19.)

Engine #18
Formerly West New York Engine 3,6, and 8
1976 Mack CF/Grumman

(Lime yellow - it was the first yellow apparatus in West New York. It was refurbished in 1985 by Grumman and returned to service painted red.)

Engine #19
Formerly Union City Engine 4
1986 Mack/Ward 79

Engine #18 1986 Mack/Ward 79

Engine #18 1976 Mack CF/Grumman

Engine #19 1986 Mack/Ward 79

North Hudson Regional Fire & Rescue Fire Companies & Units

Ladder 6 1973 Seagrave 100′ Tiller

Ladder 7 1990 Seagrave 100′ rear-mount Quint.

Ladder 7 1986 Seagrave 100′ Tiller

Spare/Reserve Apparatus

Ladder #6
Formerly Union City Truck 3, 2
1973/1990 Seagrave 100′ Tiller

Ladder #7
Formerly North Hudson Ladder 2, and Weehawken Truck 1.
1990 Seagrave 100′ rear-mount Quint.

(*First Quint in the North Hudson area.*)

Ladder #7
Formerly North Hudson Ladder 1, and Union City Truck 1.
1986 Seagrave 100′ Tiller

Ladder #7
Formerly Union City Truck 1, 3
1980 Seagrave 100′ Tiller

Ladder 7 1980 Seagrave 100′ Tiller

142 **North Hudson Regional Fire & Rescue Fire Companies & Units**

Ladder #8 1980 Seagrave rear-mount

Ladder #8 1988 Pierce 105′ Tiller

Ladder #8 1971 Howe/Duplex/Grove 100′ Tiller.

Spare/Reserve Apparatus

Ladder #8
Formerly Guttenberg Truck 1.
1980 Seagrave rear-mount

(Purchased from Glenolden Pennsylvania Fire Department, for Guttenberg, upon regionalization.)

Ladder #8
Formerly North Hudson Ladder 9, 1.
North Bergen Truck 2, Pittsburgh PA, Truck 1
1988 Pierce 105′ Tiller

Ladder #8
Formerly West New York Truck 1, 2.
1971 Howe/Duplex/Grove 100′ Tiller.
(1985 Grumman refurbished)

(Truck was loaned to Jersey City for one year as Ladder #8)

North Hudson Regional Fire & Rescue Fire Companies & Units

Formerly North Hudson Ladder 1, 2, 7 and Union City Truck 1, 1986 Seagrave 100' Tiller.

Spare/Reserve Apparatus

Ladder 9
Formerly North Hudson Ladder 1, 2, 7 and Union City Truck 1
1986 Seagrave 100' Tiller.

Ladder 9
Formerly North Bergen Truck 2, also Pittsburgh, Pennsylvania Truck 1.
1986 Pierce 105' Tiller.

(Ladder 9 was involved in an MVA, no fire fighters were injured but the tractor was destroyed. The trailer was attached to the tractor of a 1985 Seagrave (who's ladder failed load testing while assigned to Ladder1). The following year, the aerial failed it's load test, and was put out of service.)

Formerly North Bergen Truck 2, also Pittsburgh, Pennsylvania Truck 1. 1986 Pierce 105' Tiller.

Recall Apparatus

Division 2
Formerly North Hudson Car 5,
Director of Apparatus
North Bergen Car 3, Chief of Apparatus.

Division 2
Former North Hudson Battalion 3,
North Bergen Battalion Chief

Battalion 4
Formerly North Hudson Division 1,
West New York Deputy Chief.

(Both vehicles are activated after a third alarm doubtful from the Incident Commander.)

Division #2 Car

Division #2 Car

Battalion #4 Car

North Hudson Regional Fire & Rescue Fire Companies & Units 145

Repair & Transportation

The North Bergen Fleet Maintenance Shops are responsible for all repairs on fire apparatus vehicles, equipment, and SCBA.

Prior to regionalization, the North Bergen Shops were run by the Chief of Fire Apparatus. After the study that was performed to define and implement a regional Fire Department for five (5) municipalities, it was their recommendation to develop an agreement for North Bergen to provide all repairs needed for the new department.

Prior to the formation of the new Fire Department, the New Jersey Department of Personnel's requirements changed the title of the Chief of Fire Apparatus to Director of Automotive Services.

The North Bergen Fleet Maintenance/Repairs & Transportation is a Division of the North Bergen Department of Public Safety. Peter Guinchini is the Director of Automotive Services and he is responsible for the following:

- The purchase of all parts, tools and equipment to run the fleet maintenance facility
- To monitor the ordering and accounting for all parts, supplies, fuel, vehicles registrations, titles, license plates, and all mechanics, clerical staff and support personnel.
- The Director of Automotive Services reports directly to the NHRFR's two directors and the chief of department and his responsibilities include developing, specifications and purchasing of fire apparatus vehicles and support vehicles.
- Overseeing of repairing of NHRFR communication equipment, overseeing for supply and disbursing, gasoline and diesel fuel, engine oil, seven days a week for emergency vehicles.
- Providing emergency road service 24 hours a day, seven days a week.
- Checking and coordinating the performance and quality work of outside specialty contractors.
- Insuring that services and parts, equipment, or vehicles supplied, meet with the specifications required.
- Requisitioning and purchasing of all parts, and supplies of the repair shop.
- Supply mechanics and support personnel for multiple alarm fires to insure continuous operations of apparatus at fire scene.
- Disposing and auctioning of surplus vehicular apparatus.
- Complete repair of all self contained breathing apparatus testing and record keeping.
- The repair of small equipment pumps, generators, saws, fire hose and ground ladders
- Coordinate and oversee the annual testing of aerial and ground ladders.
- Coordinate and oversee the annual service testing of all fire pumping apparatus.
- Oversees seven mechanics, three laborers, and three clerical employees.

The North Hudson Regional Fire and Rescue has entered into an Interlocal Service Agreement with the Township whereas all service and supplies for the maintenance and repair of apparatus vehicles and other related fire protection equipment is charged out monthly by the Township of North Bergen to NHRFR by invoice for payment of services rendered.

Carmine Lombardo

Shops personnel in the late 1990s.

6100 Tonnelle Avenue, Building B, North Bergen

Brush Fire Unit

Auxiliary Power Unit

Field Maintenance Truck

R.A.C. Bus

Engine 5 in tow.

Repair & Transportation 147

Repair & Transportation

Shops M-2, 2006 GMC Topkick 4x4/Omaha Service Bodies

Support Service

MASK Service Unit

North Bergen O.E.M. Tanker

*Shops Repair Truck
1995 International/2008 Shops Conversion -
Ex News Delivery Truck*

148 **Repair & Transportation**

Loaner & Donated Apparatus

Engine 17, acting Fairview Engine 1

Engine 16 to Bayonne, acting Engine 1

Engine 18, as Jersey City Engine 19

Engine 17 to Dominican Republic

Loaner & Donated Apparatus 149

Honor Guard Members

Deputy Chief Nicholas Gazzillo

Captain William Demontreux

Captain Robert P. Morrison III

Captain James J. Stelman

FF Rafael Albarran

FF Luis Bodega

FF Michael Crossan

FF John E. Dorman

150 Honor Guard Members

FF Michael Flood

FF William R. Reed

FF Henry Ruiz

FF Joseph J. Rovito

FF Mihail Voicu

Honor Guard Members 151

Honorary Battalion Chiefs

Frank Baer

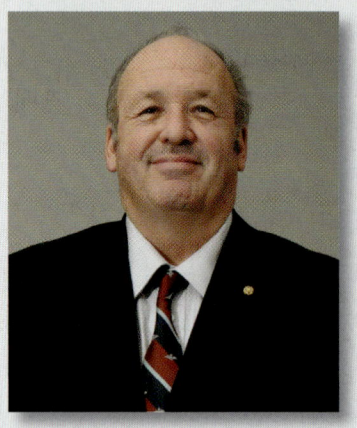

Peter Guinchini

Gary Hearn

Fred Illg

Ron Jeffers

George Steger

Mario Rossi

152 **Honorary Battalion Chiefs**

Front Pieces

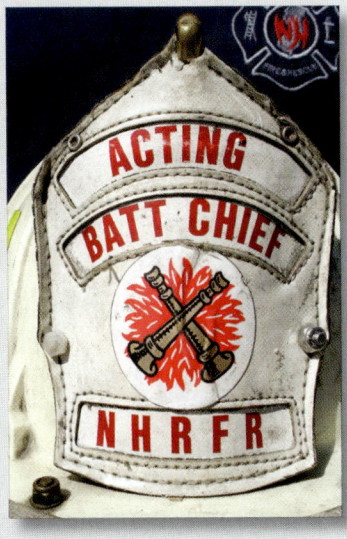

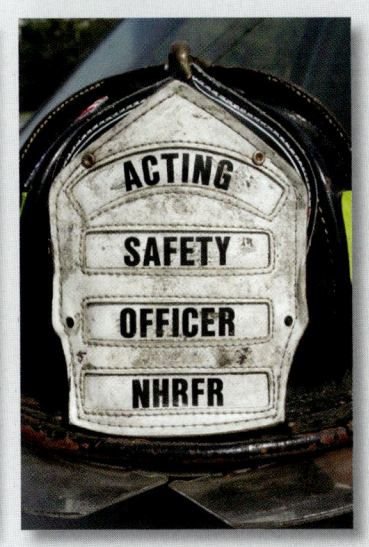

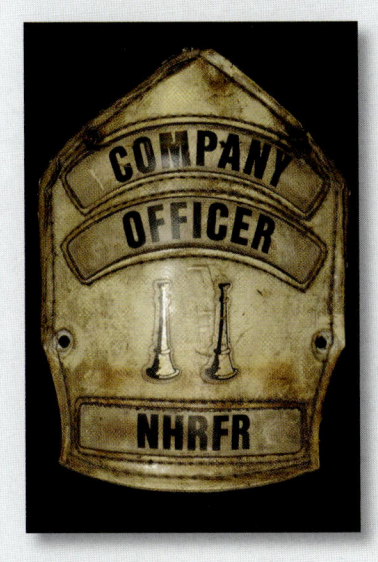

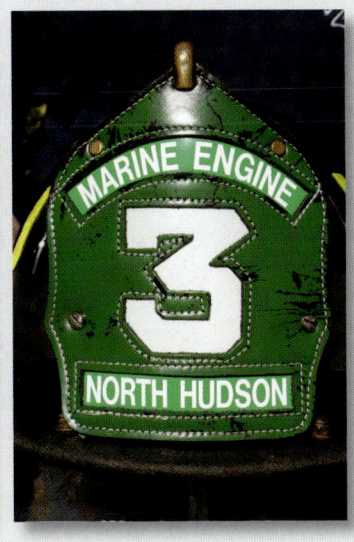

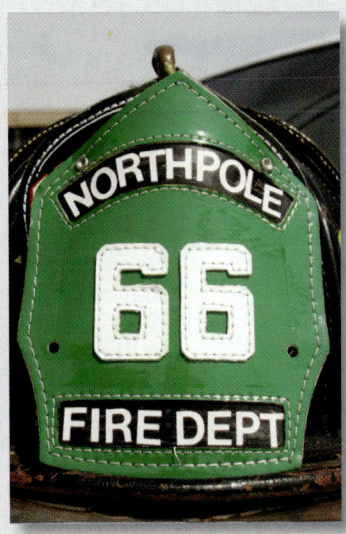

Front Pieces 153

Friends of the Fire Service

Peter Criss (KISS)

Reuben and staff from PC Richards & Sons.

Jimmy Damato and Captain Kirk Miick.

FF Brian Testino, Bobby Berger and FF Sam Griglio.

Lyndhurst FD at Wildwood Convention.

William Renner, Robert "Bobby T" Tsakarakis, and Glen Michelin.

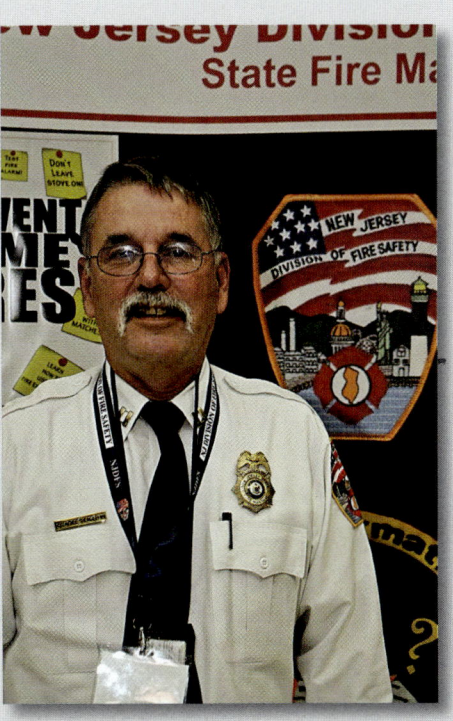

Captain Charles Luxton of NJD of FS.

N.J.D.F.S. Arson Investigation Unit Jeff Silver (left), Jason Speiker and Scout.

Bayonne Fire Canteen.

Keith Nicoliello

Tony Castillo

Visitor's from Korean Fire Department.

Friends of the Fire Service 155

Chief Presutti's Last Day

Chief Anthony Presutti began his career in the fire service in 1960 at West New York Truck 1. In 1966, he was promoted to the rank of Captain and assigned to Engine 4. He was later reassigned to Truck 1 where he would stay for 10 years.

In 1982, Chief Presutti was promoted to the rank of Deputy Chief. At that time, the Deputy rode out of Truck 1, where he was assigned for another 13 years. Chief Presutti's Deputy Aide was Firefighter Louis Kovacs, father of West New York/North Hudson Regional Captain Steven Kovacs. In 1995, he was promoted to Chief of Department. Chief Presutti spent 29 years riding out of Truck 1.

On his last day, he went back to Truck 1, which is now North Hudson Regional Fire and Rescue Ladder 4 to ride one last time. Captain Steven Kovacs gave up his officer's seat for the night to allow the Chief to ride. His chauffeur for the day was his son, Kevin Presutti and the tillerman was his nephew, Scott Morrison. Chief Presutti rode on a couple alarm activations and one full assignment before retiring after 41 years in the fire service.

Captain Robert P. Morrison III

156 Chief Presutti's Last Day

Sergeant Alvarado Serving in Iraq

Wrapping Party

In 1987, North Bergen Firefighters James Lemke (now Captain) and late Firefighter George Welch decided they wanted to do something special for sick children during the holidays. They wanted to purchase toys for hospitalized children in the local communities, so they decided to start a drive to raise money, and thus the Christmas Wrapping Party and the Hospital Visits began.

Since 1993, the driving force behind the event has been Firefighter David Velez (retired). When Regionalization took place, in 1999, Dave Velez reached out to firefighters from all of the former departments to participate in the drive, thus giving birth to the first "North Hudson Firefighters Toy Drive."

"We collect the money from the firefighters", Velez said, "All the guys chip in, as well as getting monetary donations from generous people. We then go to the store and buy the toys for the kids."

Some past and current sponsors of the Toy Drive have been, Toys R Us, Days Inn and Penske Trucking, all in North Bergen, as well, as the New Jersey Transit Garage, in Secaucus.

Some of Santa's stops for the Toy Drive include Palisades Medical Center in North Bergen, Meadowlands Hospital in Secaucus, Christ Hospital in Jersey City and Hoboken University Medical Center.

Captain James Lemke recalled some fond memories of hospital visits from the past.

"Some of the stories I can remember are when we went back the year after my daughter got out of the hospital. The first person I set my eyes on was a little three year old red headed girl who was in the hospital at the same time as my daughter the year

158 **Wrapping Party**

before. I knew it was her because my wife and I wanted to adopt her. In the month she was in the hospital the mother came only once to see her at Christmas Eve. The hospital staff told us she was better off in the hospital then home."

"Then there was another time when I caught an elderly lady out of the corner of my eye. She looked like she needed some cheering up. I called Santa into the room and took a picture with her and Santa. About two weeks later I was showing Captain Frank Montagne (now Deputy Chief) the pictures we had taken when he suddenly stopped. We had taken a picture of his grandmother who had passed away in the hospital a week earlier. This was the little elderly lady who needed some cheer."

"One year we were doing our rounds and a nurse requested that we visit an elderly lady who had taken a stroke; she said that because of the stroke, lady had not spoken for about a month, but she understood what you said to her. After the visit, I was walking out of her room when I said "Merry Christmas and May God Bless You." To the surprise of the nurse and myself she answered 'and May God Bless You.'"

"The stories go on and on and will never be forgotten. We were there to brighten all of their time in the hospitals; instead they always seemed to brighten ours. It has been about 32 years since the inception of this endeavor and about 23 years of doing it with the Fire Department," Lemke said.

The torch has been passed several times to keep the idea fresh but the event keeps getting better and better. For Captain Lemke, the miracle of his daughter being okay 32 years ago had brought him two new miracles, his grandchildren, Antonio James and Isabelle, five and two years old.

Merry Christmas to all, and to all a Good Night!

Wrapping Party 159

160 **Hospital Visits**

Hospital Visits

Hospital Visits · 161

Christmas Parade

Each year the North Hudson Regional Fire Officers and Firefighters Unions co-host a Christmas Parade down Bergenline Avenue, which is the area's largest business district. The parade runs from 83rd Street in North Bergen to 32nd Street in Union City.

"We decided to join forces and Bergenline Avenue covers the most ground," said Firefighter Glen Michelin. "We have a strong relationship with the public, and have had a lot of help from the five mayors and communities."

The Union City Fire Department started the tradition of the parade in 1971, going through their city.

"We all had our own separate parades," said retired Firefighter Billy Renner, who was with the West New York Fire Department before Regionalization in 1999. "We decided to all come together for one parade after regionalization."

Firefighter Renner has been the chairman of the Parade, since Regionalization in 1999, and continues to hold this title in his retirement.

"Billy Renner is the driving force behind this as chairman of the parade," said Captain Brian McGorty. "He contacts all kinds of people and gets the various floats and bands. Billy Renner is the Head Elf. He's done a fabulous job."

"Most often we have had very cold weather on parade day, but when you see the faces of those kids it warms everything up and makes it all worthwhile," said McGorty.

Many firefighters, who volunteer their time to march in the annual parade, bring their own families to participate each year. Many of which who are long since grown, now bring their own children.

"It's really a celebration of the relationship between our firefighters and especially the children of the community," said McGorty. "It's not only because so many of our firefighters are parents themselves, but there really is a unique relationship that exists, and any event that involves children, firefighters are willing to go that extra yard."

Major sponsors over the years have included Anpesil Candy and Hudson News Company in North Bergen; as well as Royal Printing and Rosario Starr from Perfect Party in West New York.

Another major sponsor has been Robert "Bobby T." Tsakarakis, owner of the P&L Grill located on 32nd Street in Union City, which is the ending point of the parade. Each year Bobby donates his restaurant including refreshments to the Fire Department and volunteers.

"The Christmas season brings out the best in everyone, it's a family time of year, and the fire department in itself is an extended family," said McGorty.

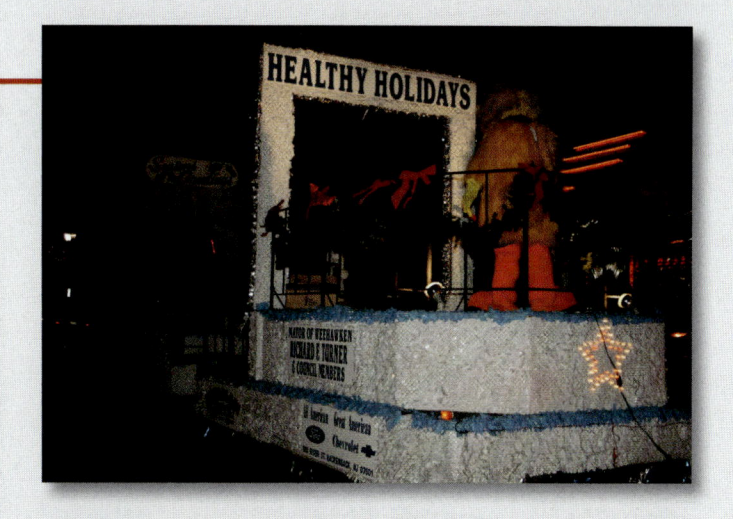

Christmas Parade

Charity Dodgeball Tournament

To help raise funds for FF Steve Hillis who was stricken with cancer.

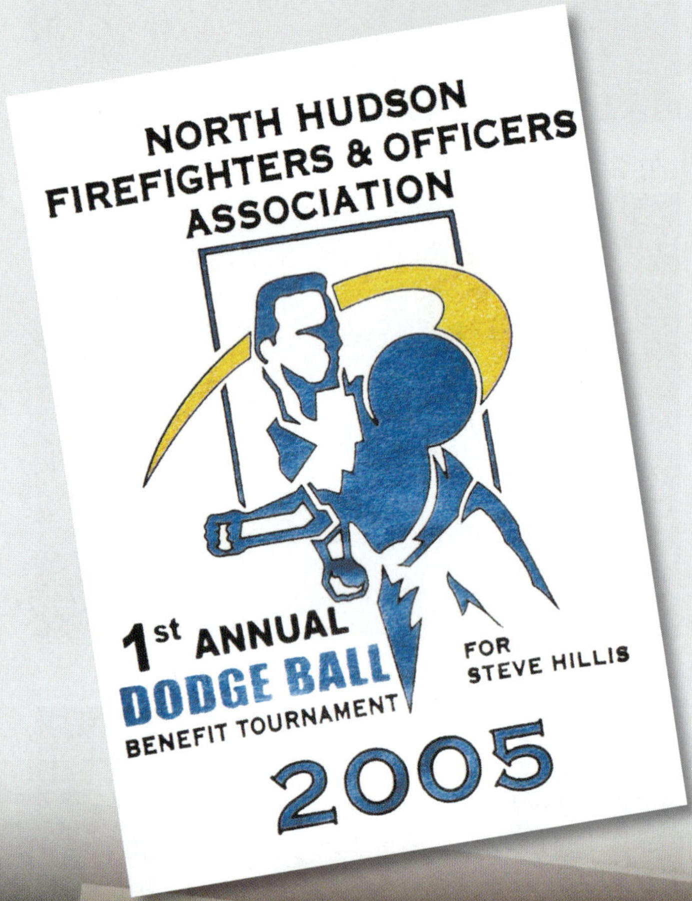

NORTH HUDSON FIREFIGHTERS & OFFICERS ASSOCIATION

1st ANNUAL DODGE BALL BENEFIT TOURNAMENT FOR STEVE HILLIS 2005

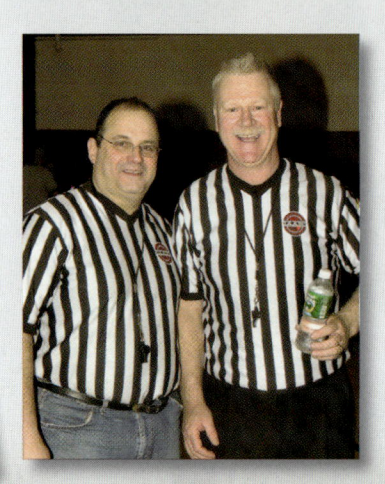

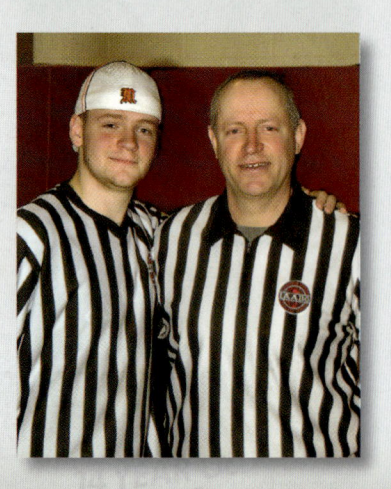

Charity Dodgeball Tournament 165

M.D.A. Boot Drive

T-Shirts For Troops

T-Shirts For Troops Project A Big Success

T-Shirts for Troops is a project that sends soldiers in Iraq shirts that show the support of New Jersey firefighters for their efforts. Plans call to extend the program to troops in Afghanistan. To date 2000 t-shirts have been sent to Iraq with another 750 getting ready for shipment.

This program was the creation of North Hudson Regional Fire Captain Kevin Moore in memory of his Godson, U.S. Army Sgt. Andrew Brown, 22, who was killed in Iraq in October, 2004.

"After the death of my Godson I came to know that these soldiers serving in harms way. Each and every one are important," Moore said. "To family, friends and loved ones."

In April, 2006, Moore met U.S. Army Chaplain Steve Walsh at the dedication of a memorial for members of the 1st Cavalry Division in Fort Hood, Texas. Captain Moore asked the chaplain the same question he had asked troops in the past, "What can you send to troops serving-what can they use?" Moore said he got pretty much the same "pat" answer, "They want for nothing-yet they appreciate everything they receive."

The chaplain continued that during his first deployment to Iraq his unit received a shipment of t-shirts. He went on to explain that you could fill a box with candy, magazines, etc., but the t-shirts were "tangible" things that soldiers could possess.

That was the beginning of T-Shirts for Troops. A shirt was designed, printed and sold to North Hudson firefighters. For each shirt sold, two are sent to soldiers in Iraq, Moore explained.

Moore, North Hudson Captain Jim Stelman and Peggy Dreker then took the project to the state level at the FMBA convention in Atlantic City. There, close to 500 shirts were sold and the project received a generous donation by the state FMBA.

The t-shirt printer was located by a fellow North Hudson firefighter. "Z-Line Imported Sportsware of Ocean Beach has been a very good friend to this effort," Moore said. "Z-Line does all of the shipping and handling for us. All we pay is the actual cost of postage to the APO."

"Firefighter John Pachone has been a great help also," Moore said. "He has picked up and delivered shirts to us which translates into more money for shirts for Iraq."

"I received my shirts and they are awesome," said SSG Quion Hall in an email to Captain Moore. "I never really realized how many people in my unit were from Jersey until I showed off the t-shirts. I really appreciate them."

"We have an overwhelming appreciation for the shirts," said SSG Mary Rose, a journalist with the 1st Cavalry Division in Baghdad.

After the most recent delivery of shirts at press time, Captain Moore received an email from Chaplain Walsh. "We received the t-shirts and there have been long lines of soldiers who want them. Once the word got out on how cool they were, the floodgates burst and I couldn't give them away fast enough!"

Captain Kevin Moore with T-Shirt.

"We are looking to make one more push to generate funds to do both the Afghanistan and Navy Seabee's in Iraq projects," Moore said.

Currently, Moore is working with the Madison Fire Department to send shirts bearing their department logo to the 10th Mountain Division in Iraq. Chief Mike Krupilis of the Middletown, Pennsylvania, Fire Department is working on a program within his department.

Anyone wanting information can check www.tshirtsfortroops.blogspot.com

("T-Shirts For Troops Project A Big Success" story submitted by Ron Jeffers, 1st Responder News)

Johnson Turner Golf Outing
To Benefit the Health and Welfare Fund

168 Johnson Turner Golf Outing

Johnson Turner Golf Outing 169

Training of the Dominican Republic Fire Department

170 Training of the Dominican Republic Fire Department

Training of the Dominican Republic Fire Department 171

NHRFR In Print

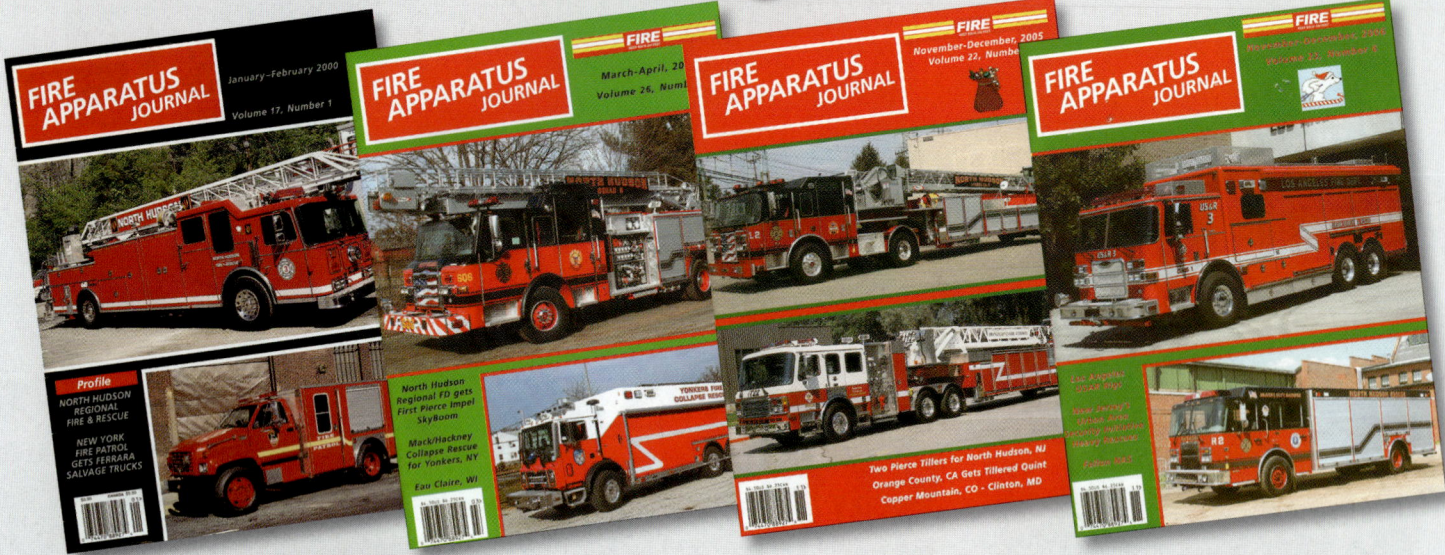

NHRFR In Print 173

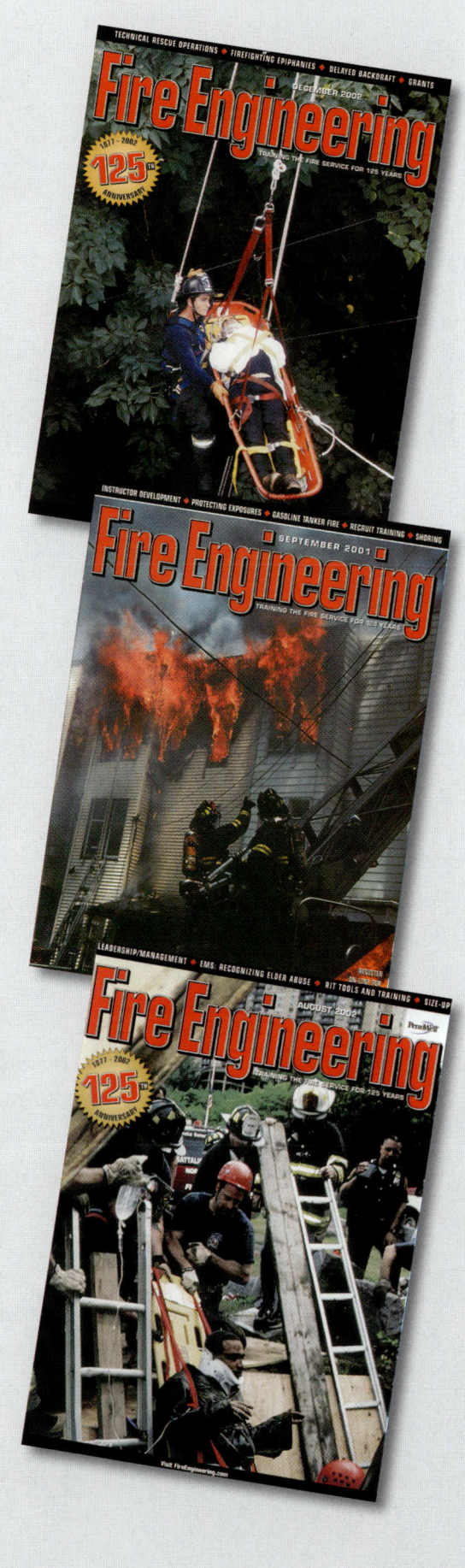

Fire Prevention

Fire Prevention 175

NHRFR Famililes

Angelo & Matthew Caliente (Father & Son)

Frank Sr., Frank Jr. & Nicholas Vasta (Father & Sons)

Peter & Patrick Cardinali (Father & Son)

Ronald & Marc A. Franco (Father & Son)

Joseph McLean III & Victor Valentin (Brother-in-Laws)

Raymond, Joseph, & Thomas Colavito (Son & Brothers)

176 NHRFR Families

David & Michael Flood (Brothers)

Mario DiPietro Sr. & Jr. (Father & Son)

Francis Jr. & Francis Sr. Baker (Father & Son)

Eugene D'Alessandro & Carmen Galese
(Son-in-Law & Father-in-Law)

Joseph McLean III & Joseph
McLean Jr. (Father & Son)

Front: Jennifer Laverty & Laura Roque
Back: Brian Barreto, David Curtis & Desmond Boyle

John, John Sr., & Michael Martin (Father & Sons)

NHRFR Families 177

Michael Jr. & Sr. Falco (Father & Son)

William & Michael Fischer (Brothers)

John & Louis Knoetig
(Father & Son)

James, Jason, and Robert Hodge
(Brothers & Nephew)

Linda & Jeffrey DiPaolo
(Mother & Son)

Joseph & Eric Inauen
(Brothers)

James, John Sr. & John Jr. Halpin
(Father & Sons)

NHRFR Families

NHRFR Families

Richard Wefer, John McCoy & Martin Mandell
(Son-in Law & Nephew)

Albert & Dominic Lorenzo
(Father & Son)

Richard Sr. & Richard Jr. Hess
(Father & Son)

Theodora & Thomas Kross
(Husband & Wife)

Michael Jr., Michael Sr., & Daniel DeOrio
(Father, Grandfather, & Son)

Robert, Peter Sr. & Peter Jr. Ellerbrock
(Brothers & Son)

Kevin and Patrick Cowan
(Brothers)

Perry & Rory Rivera
(Brothers)

Leonel & Leonard Calvo
(Brothers)

Robert & William Shelton
(Father & Son)

Jeffrey DiPaolo & John DiPaolo
(Nephew & Uncle)

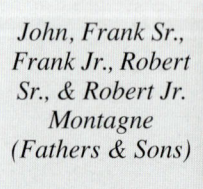

John, Frank Sr., Frank Jr., Robert Sr., & Robert Jr. Montagne
(Fathers & Sons)

180 **NHRFR Families**

NHRFR Families

The Aiello, Presutti & Morrison Families. (l. to r.) Standing: John M. Morrison, Kevin Presutti, Mark Aiello, Scott T. Morrison, Robert P. Morrison III. Seated: Anthony J. Presutti, and Robert A. Aiello.

Robert Jr., Robert Sr. & Anthony Jones
(Father & Sons)

Edward Jr. & Edward Sr. Wengerter
(Father & Son)

Terence Shevlin & Edward Flood
(Father & Son)

Timothy & Jeffrey T. Richards
(Brothers)

Kenneth, Frances, and James Furlong
(Father, Son & Uncle)

NHRFR Families 181

Frank, Samuel & Joseph Isola
(Father & Sons)

Andrew "Chicky" & Robert Pisani
(Brothers)

Randy & Brian Consentino
(Brothers)

Thomas, Debbie & Brian McGorty
(Brothers & Sister)

Robert & Glen Michelin
(Father & Son)

George & Mark Koenig
(Father & Son)

NHRFR Families

NHRFR Families

George Sr., Frank, George Jr., & Patrick Pizzuta &
Kimberley Kingsbury (Brothers, Son & Niece)

Vincent & Joseph A. Caruso
(Brothers)

Thomas & Timothy J. Steinel
(Brothers)

Walter & James Paczkowski & Richard Phalon
(Brothers & Father-in-Law)

Daniel F. & Michael J. Giacumbo
(Brothers)

Robert R. & William R. Reed
(Father & Son)

Thomas Tormey Jr. & Thomas Tormey Sr.
(Father & Son)

NHRFR Families 183

Robert & Brian Miller
(Father & Son)

Standing: George Jr. & Patrick. Seated: George Sr. & Francis Pizzuta
(Brothers & Son)

Richard Jr., Richard Sr. & David Barreres
(Brothers, Father & Sons)

Louis, Ralph & Michael Mastellone
(Father & Sons)

Charles Sr. & Charles Jr. Thomas holding Charles A. Thomas's helmet.
(Father, Son & Grandson)

William & John O'Sullivan
(Grandfather & Grandson)

NHRFR Families

NHRFR Families

Anthony Racioppi, Carmine Miceli,
& Anthony Fasciola
(Brothers & Father-in-Law)

Patrick P., Anthony Sr., and Anthony Jr. Cospito
(Father & Sons)

John E. & Brian Dorman
(Brothers)

Peter Camaiore Sr. & Jr.
(Father & Son)

Scott & Robert Morrison
(Brothers)

NHRFR Families 185

Primak & Miick Family - Thomas, Sean, William & Kirk
(Father, Son, Nephew, & Son-in-Law)

Richard Sr. & Richard Jr. Desimone
(Father & Son)

Frank Sr. and Frank Jr. Montagne
(Father & Son)

Bernice & Keith Gonyou
(Husband & Wife)

186 **NHRFR Families**

NHRFR Families

David & Michael Donnarumma
(Brothers)

Gregory & Francis W. Kemp
(Brothers)

Robert D'Antonio, Jr. & Sr.
(Father & Son)

Albie Santinello and Vincent Vacca
(Father & Son in Law)

Gazzillo & Desimone Families - Richard Sr. & Jr. & Nicholas Sr. & Jr.
(Fathers, Sons & Father-in-Law)

Richie and David Velez
(Brothers)

NHRFR Yearbook Committee

(l. to r.) Seated: Honorary Battalion Chief Ron Jeffers, Captain Robert Morrison, Kimberley Kingsbury, Battalion Chief Robert Duane, Captain Thomas Irving. Standing: Captain William Demontreux, Firefighter Joseph Candeloro, Firefighter Rafael Albarran, and Retired Firefighter David Velez.

This was a Labor of Love!

Sincerely,
The Committee

Firehouses Closed

Before this book went to print the North Hudson Fire & Rescue Management Board reduced the table of organization to 273 officers and members from 310.

At 1930 hours, June 29, 2010, Squad Company 6, Engine Company 11 and Ladder Company 2 were disbanded. At the same time, Engine Company 5's new quarters was opened at 4300 Kennedy Boulevard, Union City. Engine 5 relocated from 419-43rd Street and Rescue Company 1 was moved into this house from 6801 Madison Street, Guttenberg.

Squad 6's house at 1814-43rd Street, North Bergen, was closed. Engine 11's house, at 480-66th Street, West New York, was re-designated Supplies and Building Maintenance Division.

On July 1st, Safety 1 moved to Rescue 1's former quarters in Guttenberg and their firehouse at 133 Jane Street, Weehawken, was closed.

Battalion 2 was relocated from 4911 Broadway, West New York, to Engine 5's new quarters in Union City on July 19th.

JUNE 29, 2010

Name Index

A

Affuso 29, George 33, Tony 30
Agostini, Robert 13, 77
Ahmad, Giovanni D. 94
Aiello, Mark 181, Robert 14, 23, 25, 49, 181
Aimone, Otto 30
Albarran, Rafael 82, 150, 188
Alessi, Vincent 24
Allgeier, Joseph J. 44
Altomare, Thomas 82
Alvarado, Michael 82, 157
Alvarez, Steven 82
Amaro, Alain 82
Ambrosino, John 96
Anacker, Darren M. 82
Andes 29, Warren 26
Antommarchi, John 82
Antoncich, Rudolph S. 99
Ardito, Michael P. 99
Arena, Joseph P. 82
Arenal, Manuel 82
Astralaga, Fernando 82
Aurthur, George 97
Avello, Tony 30
Avillo, Anthony 59, 64, 73

B

Baer, Frank 96, 152
Baglino, Anthony 97
Baker, Francis Jr. 82, 177, Francis Sr. 97, 177
Baldino, Robert 99
Baldwin, Aaron 40
Ballester, Alan 25, 77
Banoff, Alexander 82
Barbanera 30
Barkus, Walter 29
Barone, Victor "Chuck" 99, 131
Barreres, David 82, 184, Richard Jr. 82, 184, Richard Sr. 97, 125, 184
Barreto, Brian 82, 177, Sergio 77
Barth 29, David 65, 72, Donald 26
Baxes, Gustavo 97, 131
Beadle, Edward A. 36, 38, 39
Becker 29, Andy 30, Frankie 33
Becket, Ernest G. 23
Bender, James 97
Berger, Bobby 154
Bergman 29
Bielka, John 33
Bodega, Luis 82, 150
Bodziak, Damon 83
Boele 29, Brian 10, 33, 77, Hank 32
Bolte, George 38
Borbon, Juan 95
Boyle, Desmond 83, 177
Braddock, James J. 31
Brander, George 99
Broking, Scott M. 77
Brown, Andrew 167
Browne, George 99
Burlingame, Charles 59, Wendy 59

C

Cabral, Robert 50, 99
Cahill 42
Caliente, Angelo 97, 176, Matthew 83, 176, Michael 99
Calvo, Leonard 77, 180, Leonel 77, 125, 180
Camaiore, Peter Jr. 77, 185, Peter Sr. 185
Candeloro, Joseph 76, 188
Canetti, Brian 32, 99
Cannon, Robert 97
Cardinali, Patrick 77, 176, Peter 176
Carpenter, Vic 29
Caruso, Joseph A. 83, 183, Vincent 83, 183
Casey 29
Casper, Anthony S. 83
Castillo, Tony 155
Cavanaugh, Edward 25
Cellini, Rudy 33
Cervate, Robert 38
Chinea 38
Chrissakis, Steven 99
Ciavatta, Robert A. 99
Cocciadiferro, Kory 83, Michael 83
Cody, Alan 29, 32, 76, 131
Colacci, Timothy 83
Colavito 39, Joseph 39, 176, Raymond 39, 83, 176, Robert 39, Thomas 39, 176
Collette, Michael 97
Columbie, Mercedes 96
Concepcion, Jaime 83
Connors, Edward 77
Conroy, Vincent 32
Consentino, Brian 182, Randy 182
Corbo, Kevin 83
Corso, James 83
Cosentino, Brian 83, 125, Randy J. 76
Cospito 29, Anthony 77, Anthony Jr. 185, Anthony Sr. 185, Patrick 83, 185
Cowan 29, Kevin 33, 83, 180, Patrick 84, 180
Crandal, Frank 38
Cranwell, Michael 14, 64, 67, 75, 131, Philip 84
Crispino, Christopher J. 99
Criss, Peter 154
Crossan, Michael 84, 150
Curley, Damon 84
Curtis 66, David 64, 73, 177

D

Dabal, Michael 94
D'Alessandro, Eugene 84, 177
Daley, John J. 44
Damato 29, Jimmy 154, Mark 84
D'Antonio 29, Robert Jr. 84, 187, Robert Sr. 97, 187
Defina, Angelo 99
DeLeo 29, 32
Deleon, Rafael 99
Delgado, Jorge 84
Dembroe, Alan 77
Demontreux, William 42, 54, 77, 150, 188
Dempsey, William Jr. 84
Denzler, David 97
DeOrio 29, Daniel 29, 84, 179, Michael 29, 49, 94, 179
DeSavino, Howie 32
Desimone 187, Richard Jr. 84, 186, Richard Sr. 77, 186
DeVito 39, Philip 39
Diaz, Eduardo L. 77
DiGiammo, Theodore 33
Dilworth, James 97
DiPaolo, Jeffrey 84, 178, 180, John 26, 180, Linda 28, 94, 178
DiPietro, Mario Jr. 177, Mario Sr. 177
DiStefano 31, Pete 26
Ditursi, John "Butch" 32, 33
DiVincent 29, Guy 32, Joe 32
Donnarumma 29, David 32, 72, 187, Michael 84, 187
Donnelly, James J. 78
Dorman, Brian 185, John 84, 125, 150, 185
Dragona, Anthony 39
Dreker, Peggy 167
Drimones, George 38
Duane, Robert 6, 10, 54, 75, 188
Duque, Orlando 96
Dvorak 29, Bernie 30, Frank 29

E

Ebel, Edward 33
Eckrote, John 97
Eits, J. E. 43
Eller, Andy 33
Ellerbrock, Peter Jr. 179, Peter M. 84, Peter Sr. 179, Robert 97, 179
Estabrook, Robert 38, Todd 84

F

Falco 29, Michael 74, Michael Jr. 178, Michael Sr. 33, 178
Falk, Harold 99
Fasciola, Anthony 185
Fede, Fred 78
Ficken, Charles E. 85, Raymond 50, 99
Finkeldey, Gary 96
Firtion, Tim 96
Fischer 29, Michael 15, 32, 33, 178, William 72, 178
Flood, David 78, 125, 177, Edward 11, 51, 53, 69, 97, 125, 181, Michael 85, 151, 177
Flora, Carmine 15
Floriani, Steve 32
Focht, Robert L. 99
Franco, Marc A. 78, 176, Ronald 176
Franke 29, George Jr. 30, 99, George Sr. 26
Fresse, Daniel 85
Friedel, George C. 38
Furlong, Frances 181, James 85, 181, Kenneth 181

G

Galese, Carmen 97, 177
Gallagher 29, Frank 85, John 99, Rich 32
Garrity, Doug 30
Gavin, Glen 85
Gaynor, Thomas "Tacky" 29
Gazzillo 29, 187, Nicholas 32, 57, 73, 150
Gerard, Frank 43
German, Merlin 128
Gerrity, Mitchell D. 85
Giacumbo 67, Daniel F. 74, 183, Michael 65, 72, 183
Gibb, Steven J. 99
Gigante, Vito 85
Guinchini, Peter 49, 96, 131, 146
Gobin, Joseph 85
Gonyou, Bernice 186, Keith 78, 131, 186
Gora, Richard 85, 125
Gorden, Henry J. 43
Granata, Harold J. Jr. 99
Griglio, Samuel 85, 154
Groggins, Edward 38
Grome, Richard 95
Guinchini, Pete 124, 152
Guth, William 32
Gutierrez, Jose 85
Gutjahr, Herman 29, 33, John 29
Guzzo, Albert P. 99

H

Haemmerle, Steven 85, Thomas 85
Hall, Quion 167
Halpin, James 85, 178, John Jr. 75, 178, John Sr. 178
Hamel 29
Hamlin, Chauncey 32
Hanford, Walter 99
Hargaden, James 26, 32, 33
Hearn, Gary 57, 152,
Hegarty, Stephen J. 78
Heitmann, Ron 28
Hermann, F. W. 43
Hernandez, Carlos 85
Hern, Michael 78, 125
Hess, Richard J. 78, Richard Jr. 179, Richard Sr. 179
Heydorn, Arthur 99
Hickey, John 96

Hillis, Steven 86, 164
Hislop, Ruben 86
Hodge, James 97, 178, Jason 86, 178, Robert 97, 178
Holling 29, Donald "Red" 32
Hone, John F. 86
Hoover, Thomas 99
Huelbig, Matthew 86, Thomas 86

I

Illg, Fred 152
Inauen, Eric 68, 69, 97, 178, Joseph 178
Incognito, Luke 99
Indri, Alec 86
Indri, Marco 78
Inzerillo, Leonard 38, 99
Ippolito, Gary 33, 97
Irving, Steven P. 86, Thomas 28, 32, 33, 76, 188
Isola, Frank 182, Joseph F. 78, 182, Samuel L. 78, 182
Izquierdo, Jose 86

J

Jackson, Andrew 42, Kevin 28, 86
Jauregui, Juan 98
Jeffers, Ron 12, 17, 19, 25, 39, 54, 152, 167, 188
Johnson, Marc 33, 75
Jones, Anthony 78, 181, Noreen Mimi 95, Robert 49, 51, Robert Jr. 86, 181, Robert Sr. 11, 98, 181
Jorquera, Christian 86

K

Kandrac, Ken 98
Keenan, Patrick 32, 33
Kelly, Frank B. 44, John A. 99, Simon 40, Thomas E. 99
Kemp, Francis W. 187, Gregory 86, 125, 187
Kingsbury, Kimberley 7, 12, 54, 94, 183, 188
Kirchoff, Paul 78
Kiszka, Frank Jr. 78
Klein, Charles 43, Herman 43, Matthias 43
Knoetig, John 98, 178, Louis 86, 178

Koenig, George 182, Mark 86, 182
Korn, Barney 38
Kovacs, Louis 156, Steven 99, 156
Kraemer, Fred W. 44
Krieger, William 86
Kritsky, Joseph 99
Kross, Theodora 94, 179, Thomas 87, 179
Krupilis, Mike 167

L

Laban, William 78
Lacarubba, David 87
Lacenere, Michael 95
Lahres, D. Joseph 44
Lambert, Frank X. 44
Lang 29, George J. 76
Laterra, Richard 74
Lavelle, Joseph 32, 98
Laverty, Jennifer 95, 177
Lavin, William J. 9
Lavino, Auggie 30
Leahy 29, Dave 33
Leao, Edward 87
Leaycraft, Frederick 87
Lehnes 29
Lemke, James 32, 79, 158
Lemonie, William J. 79
Leon, Ramon 87
Liberti, Daniel 87
Liberton, Joseph 25
Licini, Angelo M. 87
Lisa, James 87
Lombardi, John 96
Lombardo, Carmine 146, Marc 87
Lopez, Paul 87
Lordo, Michael 87
Lorenz, Mark R. 79
Lorenzo, Albert 179, Dominic 79, 179
Lucia, Anthony 87
Lurcott, Alfred 43
Lurig 29
Luxton, Charles 155

M

Magnuson, Robert 32
Maher, James H. 87
Majors, Alexander 87
Malik, Thomas J. 87
Mancini, Peter 87, 125
Mandell, Martin 98, 179
Marino, Dominick 8, 88, Don 32, 33

Marione, Scott 32, 79, 125
Markou, Markos 99
Martin 29, John Jr. 177, John Sr. 177, Michael 79, 177
Martinez, Alexander 99, Francisco D. 88, Frank 67
Mastellone, Louis 184, Michael 88, 184, Ralph 98, 184
Masterson, Mark E. 79
Mastro, Eugene La 78
Mathioudakis, Nick 88
McCabe, Mickey 65
McCann, Brian T. 88
McCoy, John 179
McDonough, James 79
McEldowney, Brion 5, 17, 53, 56, 64, 72, Daniel 88
McGauley, Steve 32
McGorty, Brian 10, 76, 162, 182, Debbie 182, Thomas 182
McLaughlin, Joseph A. 26
McLean, Joseph III 88, 176, 177, Joseph Jr. 15, 177
McLellan, James 98, Sean T. 79
McMains, James 98
McMonegal 30
Meckert, Adolph 43
Melendez, Luis 88, 125
Mellifiore, Ronald 99
Mennitto, Gary 88, 125
Menzel 30
Mezzina, Keith 88, 125
Miceli, Carmine 185
Michelin, Glen 9, 39, 88, 155, 162, 182, Robert 38, 39, 182
Mier, Raul 88
Miick 186, Kirk 32, 54, 79, 154, Sean 13, 79, 125
Miller, Brian 88, 184, Calvin 99, Frank 28, 32, Robert 184, William 95
Mirabelli, Steven 99
Mitarotonda, Nicola Jr. 88
Mitchell, Alfred R. 99
Mohr, Denise 96
Montagne 29, 32, 58, Bob 29, Frank 29, 30, 51, 59, 73, 125, 126, 159, Frank "Fish" 29, Frank Jr. 180, 186,

Frank Sr. 180, 186, John 29, 98, 99, 180, Robert 98, Robert Jr. 180, Robert Sr. 180
Moore, John 88, Kevin 98, 99, 167
Morales, Luis F. 88
Moran 30
Morrison, John M. 181, Robert P. III 12, 25, 54, 79, 125, 150, 156, 181, 185, 188, Scott 89, 156, 181, 185
Motta, Mike 32
Munafo, Eugene R. 89
Mureo, Gary R. 79
Murphy 29, James 32

N

Nacca 29, Patty 32
Nagurka, Frank 38
Neglia, Vincent 12, 15, 16, 17, 32, 51, 53, 127
Newcomb, Drew C. 79
Nichols, Richard 89
Nicoliello 30, Keith 28, 155
Noble, Charlie 28
Noe, George 33
Notaro, Gianni 89, Salvatore 89
Notre, Brian T. 89
Novembre, Anthony 38, Michael 89

O

O'Brien, James 29
O'Driscoll, Kevin 15
O'Neil, William 42
Oriente, Michael 57, 74
Ortiz, Roberto 89
O'Sullivan, John 79, 184, William 184

P

Pabon, Sonia 94
Pachone, John 167
Pachon, John 89
Paczkowski, James 183, Richard 98, Walter 79, 183
Pallotta, Nicholas 32, 98
Palmer, David 99, Robert 89
Palombini, John 99
Pantaleo, Al 33
Pearce, David E. 89
Peek, Deborah 95
Pelletreau, Robert 24
Pena, Elvis 89

Peralta, Rafael 89
Percuoco, John R. 89
Perez, Alain 89, Carlos 89, Ivan 99
Peschetti, Daniel 96, Steve 96
Peters, Herman 80, Paul 99
Pfeifer, George 98
Phalon, Richard 183
Pieretti, John 99
Pietro, Mario Di Jr. 77
Pisani, Andrew 182, Robert 80, 182
Pizzo, Iggy 33
Pizzuta, Frank 183, 184, George Jr. 98, 183, 184, George Sr. 183, 184, Patrick 98, 183, 184
Polcari, Stephen P. 80
Porta, John 99, 131
Postorino 29
Prato, Nicholas 90
Pratts, Alider 90
Preciose, Richard 99, 131
Prellberg, Alan R. 99
Presutti, Anthony 11, 23, 24, 25, 49, 51, 98, 156, 181, Kevin 90, 156, 181
Primak 186, Thomas 90
Prina, George G. 90
Prisco, Richard A. 90
Promersperger, John 38
Provede, John 38
Prunes, Adrian 90
Pucher, Frank 98
Pujols, Jose 90

Q

Quidor, Steven 74
Quigley, Joseph 98, 99
Quinn, Edward 32, 90

R

Racioppi, Anthony 33, 90, 185
Ramos, Jose 90
Raparelli, Brian 90
Rausch 29
Reck, Wilbur 30
Reed, Robert R. 72, 183, William 90, 125, 151, 183
Rehfeld, Markus 90
Renner, William 90, 99, 155, 162
Reo, Anthony J. 90
Repetti, Daniel 99
Richards, Jeffrey T. 91, 181, Timothy 91, 181

Name Index 191

Name Index

Every Fireman's Dream

Riley, Kevin 32, 80
Ring, William J. 80
Ritchie, Donald J. 99
Rivera, Perry 76, 180, Rory 80, 180
Rizzo, Jack 91
Rodriguez, Jose 80
Romano, Robert L. 99, Susie 29
Romer, Gene 30, 32
Roque, Laura 95, 177
Roselle, James 28, 30
Rose, Mary 167
Rossi, Mario 39, 152
Rovito, Dominic 32, 80, Joseph J. 91, 151
Royce, Charles 38
Rudd, Dennis J. 80
Ruggiero, Frankie 30
Ruiz, Henry 91, 151
Ruocco, Domenico 99
Rush 29, Donald 32, Jonathan 80

S

Saber, Louis 99
Salvesen, Albert 91
Santoniello, Albie 30, 32, 33, 187
Sanzari, Martin 76
Schack, Dennis 30
Schlaffer, Carlos 80
Schmelz, Frank 24
Schneider, Albert 23
Schriever, John 99
Schulz, Joseph 44
Schwartz, Thomas 33, 91
Schwartzmeier, Joseph 43
Scott, Andrew 95
Scura, Robert 91
Severino, Charles 32, 33, 99
Sharp, William Jr. 91
Sharples, Thomas M. 91
Shelton, Robert 180, William 91, 180
Shevlin, Terence C. 91, 181
Shopmann, Willy 32
Sibani, Jason 91
Sico, Dominic 76, 131
Silver, Jeff 155
Silvero, Frank 95
Sisserson, Robert 99
Sissick, Chris M. 91
Smayda, Michael 96, 99
Smith 29, Charles F. 23, Curtis 30, Tommy 30
Snyder, Charles 91
Soimes, Stuart M. 91
Speiker, Jason 155
Stack, Brian 18
Stahl 29, Brian G. 92, Harry 31
Stankard 29
Stanke, Gary Stoch 99
Steger, George 152
Steinel 29, Charles 99, Thomas 32, 92, 183, Timothy 32, 80, 183
Steiner 29
Stelman, James J. 10, 80, 150, 167
Stewart, Robert W. 99
St. James, Dennis 99
Stolc, William 92
Sullenberger, Chesley B. 65
Sullivan 29, Sean 44, 80
Supel, Robert 30

T

Taormina, Robert 99
Tardio 38
Testa, Richard 80
Testino, Brian 92, 154
Teta 29, Glenn W. 92, Thomas 99
Tholen, Ronald 99
Thomas, Charles 29, Charles A. 184, Charles Jr. 33, 184, Charles R. 75, Charles Sr. 33, 184
Tierney, Robert 99
Todd, Kevin M. 92
Tolomeo, James 99
Tompkins, Ron 99, 131
Toomey, John 92
Tormey, Thomas Jr. 80, 183, Thomas Sr. 183
Torre, Tom 30
Torres, Robert Jr. 92
Trujillo, Orlando 92
Tsakarakis, Robert "Bobby T." 155, 162
Tubby, Bruce 99
Turner 29, Glenn 33, 92

U

Umhoefer, E. 43

V

Vacca, Louis 94, Vincent 92, 187
Vagts, Drew D. 92
Valdes, Moises 81
Valdivia, Eduardo 92
Valente, Emil L. 99
Valentin, Victor 92, 176
Valentine, William 65, 75
Valenzuela, Raymond 92
Vangelakos, Victor 81
Van Leuven, Thomas G. 92
Vanore, Ralph 33
Vargas, Alfredo Jr. 93, Jose A. 93
Vassallo, Stefan 33, 93
Vasta 29, Frank A. 74, Frank Jr. 33, 176, Frank Sr. 33, 176, Nicholas 32, 93, 176
Velez 29, David 12, 32, 99, 158, 187, 188, Richie 93, 187
Veltre, Johnathan 96
Venezia, Anthony 81, 125
Ventura, Brent 93
Viccaro, George 26
Victor 176
Viscardo 29, Daniel Jr. 32, 99, Daniel Sr. 29, 32, 33
Voicu, Mihail 93, 151
Voorhis, William 24

W

Walsh, Steve 167
Watson, Eugene 96
Wefer, Richard 93, 179
Welch, George 32, 158
Welz, Jeffery 16, 49, 66, 94
Wengerter, Edward 99, Edward Jr. 93, 181, Edward Sr. 181
Wernli 29
Wertz, J. H. 43
Westphal, Larry 30
Whelan, Jack 30
Whitman, Christie 49
Wilcomes 29
Willard, William G. 93
Willbergh, Thomas 93
William, Alan Jr. 93
Williams 29
Williamson, Donald 32, 99
Wilson, Bruce 99, Erik 93
Winters, Eric 81
Wojtowicz, Steven 93
Woltmanm, William C. 81
Woltmann, John E. 81

Z

Zahn 29, George L. 99
Zampella, Ron 33
Zavardino, Joseph 17, 33, 99
Zell, Frank 23
Zerquera, Rodolfo 95
Zoetjes, Joanne 96

192 **Name Index**